North To The Horizon

North To The Horizon

Searching For Peary's Crocker Land

Harrison J. Hunt, M.D. and Ruth Hunt Thompson

All photographs in this book are courtesy of the American Museum of Natural History

Down East Books Camden, Maine

ISBN 0-89272-080-8
Library of Congress Catalog Number 80-69081

Down East Enterprise, Inc., Camden, Maine
Printed in the United States of America

to all who travel awhile on an empty stomach,
and keep a steady heart and a firm mouth

Preface

THEY CHASED a will-o'-the wisp, my father and six other rugged young men. They went searching for a fabled land in unexplored territory far north of the known world. They were the last of the great American Arctic exploring expeditions to depend entirely on the feet of man and dog to stretch man's knowledge of his earth, the last to know and live with an Eskimo tribe still in the stone age, surviving against the hardest climate on earth. As far as I have been able to ascertain, my father was the first physician to travel the territory of that nomadic tribe, the Polar Eskimos, in order to treat their ills, and he traveled it by dog sledge.

On July 2, 1913, Harrison J. (Hal) Hunt, MD sailed from Brooklyn on the steamship *Diana* as surgeon of the Crocker Land Expedition to the North Polar Regions, under the auspices of the American Museum of Natural History and the American Geographical Society, with the cooperation of the University of Illinois, and led by Donald B. (Mac) MacMillan.

The expedition was expected to last two years, but for two years the relief ship failed to reach them, so in the fourth winter, 1916-1917, Hal was ordered to South Greenland by dog sledge and thence to Denmark by ship, to insist that an able relief ship be sent to Etah in time the following summer to bring the remainder of the expedition home. W. Elmer Ekblaw, who accompanied him as far as South Upernavik from Umanak (now Dundas, near Thule Air Force Base), wrote of Hal's trip:

> Because of thin ice, he was forced to go by an entirely new route, directly back over the mountains. The story of his successful journey south is an epic, a record of success over incredible difficulties, and dauntless perseverance in the face of almost insurmountable obstacles. [1]

Hal learned the language of the Polar Eskimos well enough for all necessary practical purposes. He traveled a good 3,000 miles with them, lived in the igloos with them, went hungry with them. It was not in his contract to treat the Eskimos, but he was eager to do so. When he heard of a sick child, he drove a dog sledge 150 miles to see him. They called him *Nagorsakswa,* big doctor, or *Nanookswa,* big bear. He became an *angekok,* their big medicine man.

Hal, thirty-five years old, was chosen for the expedition not only for his medical skill but also for his leadership qualities, his excellent physique, and his resourcefulness. Mac knew him when Hal was at Bowdoin College and the only man in the history of the college to be captain of both the football team and the track team. Once when faced with a muddy football field and inadequate shoes, Hal cut up a garden hose to make cleats for the team, and they literally ran to victory. Later, as a young doctor faced with a premature baby in a remote farmhouse, he popped the baby into the open oven of the kitchen stove. The baby thrived.

Doctor and athlete, Hal was also an expert hunter, angler, canoeist, sailor, archer, and chess player.

He had other characteristics which lay behind his decision to leave for two years in the Arctic and behind both his success and his disillusionment while there. He enjoyed solitude, particularly in the woods. He also enjoyed people, with whom he was quiet and low-keyed, unless his sense of honesty and fair play was challenged or his sense of humor triggered. He took his friends to remote fishing holes, and if there was one other canoe there, he found the place too crowded and was ready to return home, and return home they did.

Sometimes his resourcefulness seemed too casual. He never carried a setting pole for poling up fast water or guiding the canoe slowly down rock-strewn rapids. When in need of one he cut a stiff sapling that would serve, though it would not be properly shod with a metal tip. After the evening meal at camp, the dog cleaned the frypan, which was often all the washing it got. In the morning Hal threw in enough thick slabs of bacon and flipped enough pancakes to last all day. For lunch, out of his pocket came the cold bacon wrapped in the cold pancakes. If he could make do, so could we, though he was far more thoughtful of our comfort than of his own. For himself he seemed unmindful of discomfort or hardship. When he told me that he had been afraid of the cold before he went north, I was astonished.

Hal went his own way, and his own way was straight ahead. He did not compromise gracefully. In later years, as he grew deaf, if something he was hearing went against the grain, he just turned off his hearing aid. Habitually, whatever was in his way he ignored or removed with dispatch. When, off the coast of Maine, the lead centerboard of his motorsailer, the *Ahab*, banged in a seaway, he cut it loose, all five hundred dollars' worth, and the *Ahab* became a motorboat. When he wished to leave for the Arctic, he ignored the dismay of his wife, Marion, and their financial difficulties, just as he had ignored them when, newly wed, all they had to eat were the potatoes and carrots with which his latest patient — and patients were scarce at first — had paid him. However strapped they were, he never sent a bill. To those who praised his selflessness, he chuckled and allowed it was really laziness. His modesty was such that he would have considered the publication of this book foolishness.

Hal's wife, Marion, was a city girl whose family had had to struggle to make ends meet, so she longed for security. Hal was at heart a country man, a wilderness man, who let nature take its course. He would have been happy to give away all he had and live from day to day and hand to mouth as circumstances might permit. Happily for all concerned, Marion, who had been a mathematics major at Radcliffe, was as practical as Hal was impractical about money matters, and she took over the family finances. She was a strong-minded, practical woman, and in small things she bossed him unmercifully. Yet she spent her life trying, often not very successfully or happily, to understand him, to adjust her ways to his, and to shield them both from the extremes of his temperament.

Hal was always pondering what lay over the edge of life's horizons. He sought fine views, sunsets, moonlit nights, but he did not talk about them. I do not remember his speaking, as others have, of the beauty and majesty of the Northlands. He enjoyed music, loved poetry, and often quoted it. A slim volume of Robert Browning's poems accompanied him to Greenland and back again, even when he was traveling light with just a sleeping bag and extra footwear. He was a romantic, and he sought adventure.

Hal went on the Crocker Land Expedition against the wishes of his father, Walter Lowrie Hunt, MD, of Bangor, Maine, and despite the grief of his wife. The loneliness that began in her when he announced his plans never left her. This grief and loneliness he never fully perceived. He headed north driven by an impulsive desire to visit the rim of the world, a desire in harmony with his intense professional dedication.

Here is Hal's account of his four years in Greenland and Ellesmere Land.[2] For six months he kept a diary; on some trips he made field notes; upon his return he wrote little, and only for the family. He gave few interviews, few lectures, but for the rest of his life these years remained with him in vivid detail. As he told of them to family and friends by the fireside, he left for the Arctic regions and took his listeners with him. Sometimes immediately afterwards my mother went off to her typewriter, and I thank her for her notes. Sometimes he allowed us to turn on the tape recorder.

I have used Hal's diaries and memories to make a patchwork quilt. Just as my ancestors chose and featherstitched pieces of fine satin and velvet to construct a quilt, so have I arranged the pattern, and cut and stitched together these pieces, these diaries and memories that describe Hal's life in the far north.

RUTH HUNT THOMPSON
Hancock, Maine

[1]Donald B. MacMillan, *Four Years in the White North* (New York, 1918). Appendix III, by W. Elmer Ekblaw.

[2]Ellesmere Island, referred to as Ellesmere Land by Hunt and by MacMillan in *Four Years in the White North.*

Contents

Illustrations

All poetry quoted in this book is from the poem "The Feet of the Young Men," by Rudyard Kipling.

North To The Horizon

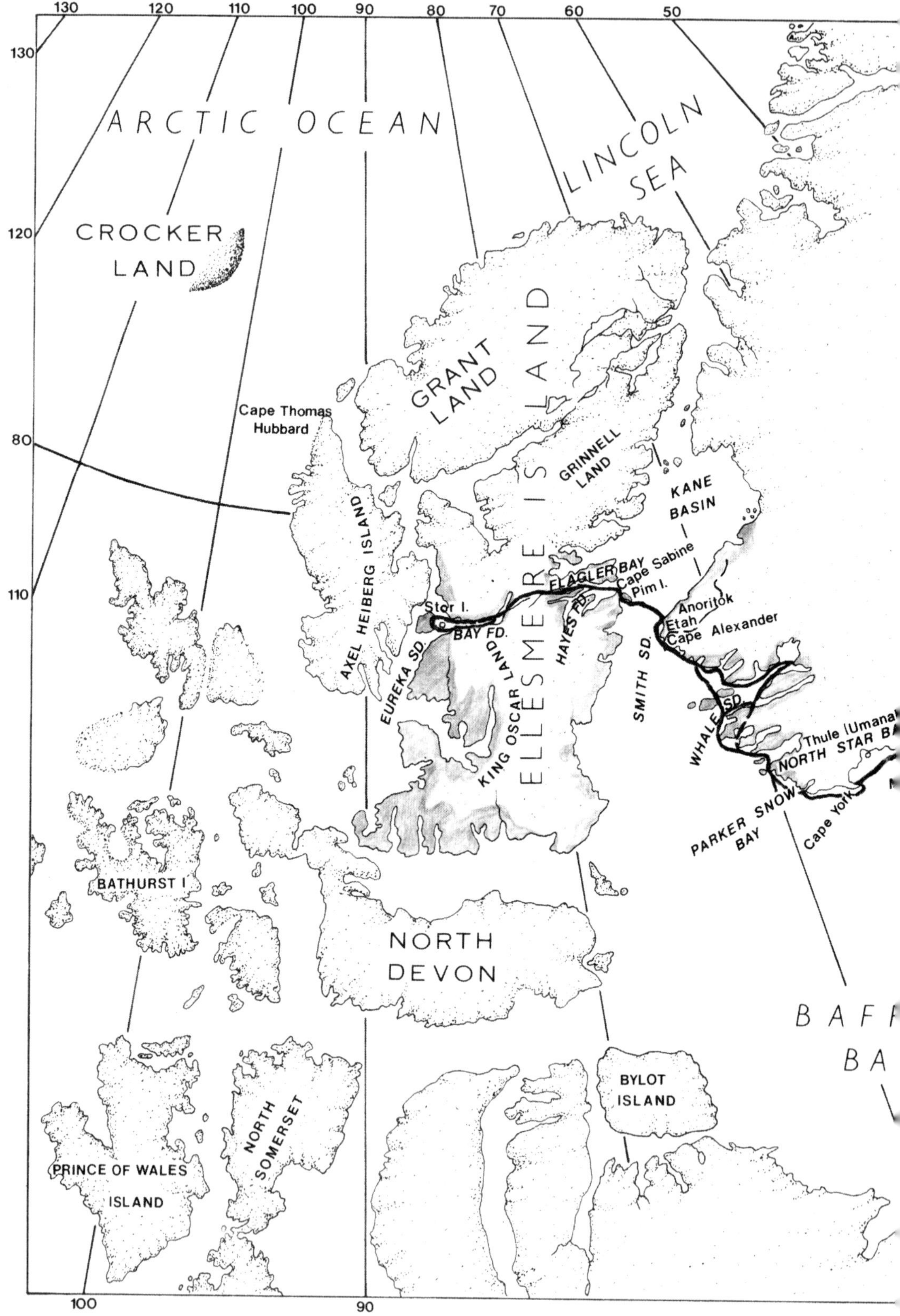
ARCTIC OCEAN
LINCOLN SEA
CROCKER LAND
GRANT LAND
ELLESMERE ISLAND
GRINNELL LAND
KANE BASIN
Cape Thomas Hubbard
AXEL HEIBERG ISLAND
FLAGLER BAY
Cape Sabine
Pim I.
Stor I.
BAY FD.
HAYES FD.
Anoritok
Etah
Cape Alexander
EUREKA SD.
KING OSCAR LAND
SMITH SD.
WHALE SD.
Thule (Umanak)
NORTH STAR BAY
PARKER SNOW BAY
Cape York
BATHURST I.
NORTH DEVON
BYLOT ISLAND
NORTH SOMERSET
PRINCE OF WALES ISLAND
BAFF
BA
130
120
110
100
90
80
70
60
50
130
120
80
110
100
90

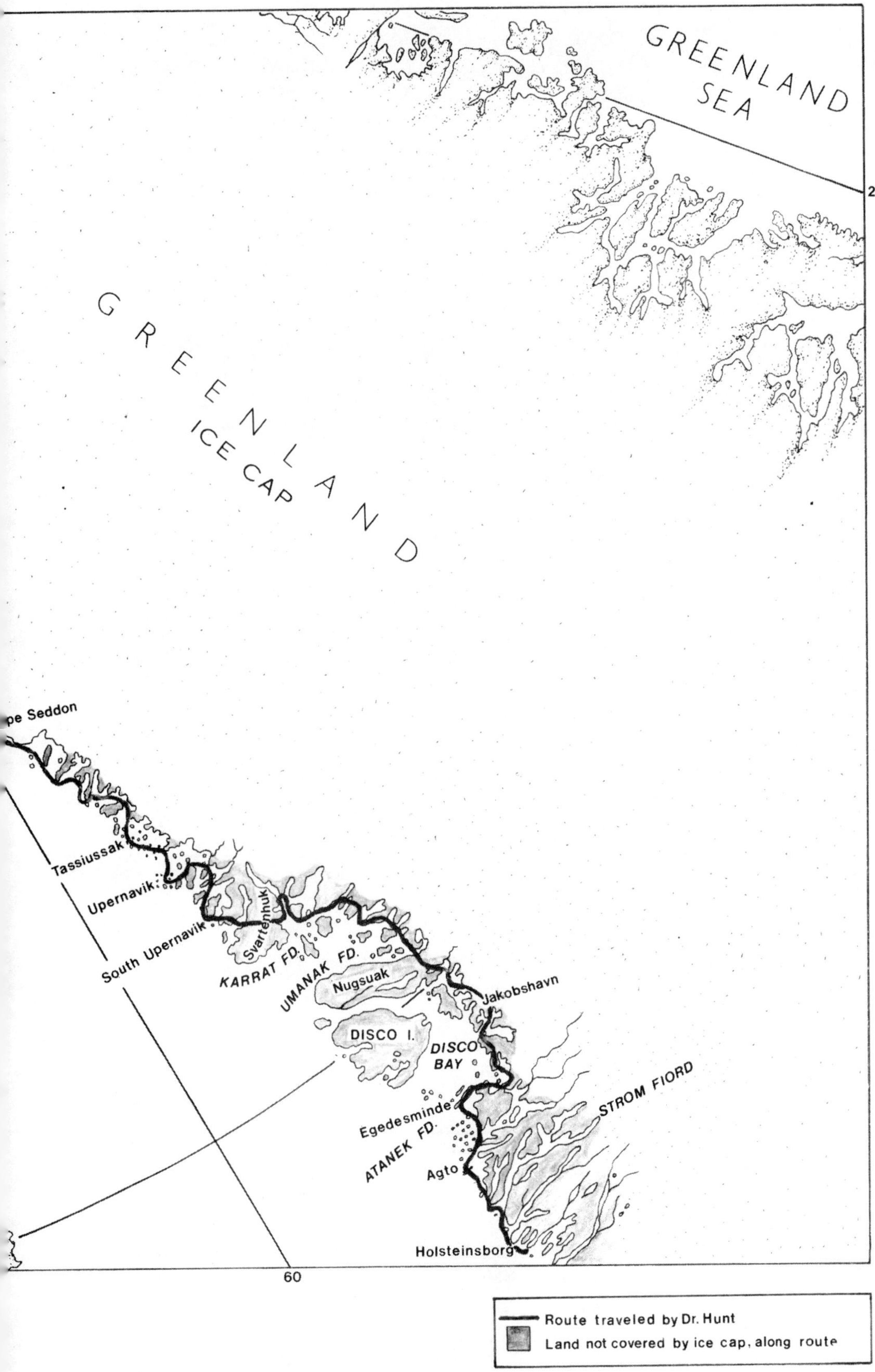

GREENLAND SEA
20
GREENLAND
ICE CAP
pe Seddon
Tassiussak
Upernavik
South Upernavik
Svartenhuk
KARRAT FD.
UMANAK FD.
Nugsuak
Jakobshavn
DISCO I.
DISCO BAY
STROM FIORD
Egedesminde
ATANEK FD.
Agto
Holsteinsborg
60
Route traveled by Dr. Hunt
Land not covered by ice cap, along route

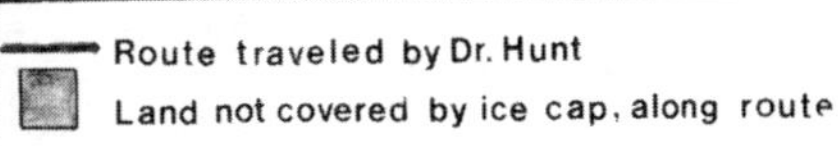

I

The Crocker Land Expedition

Now the Four-way Lodge is opened, now the Hunting Winds are loose —
Now the Smokes of Spring go up to clear the brain;
Now the Young men's hearts are troubled for the whisper of the Trues,
Now the Red Gods make their medicine again!

• • • •

He must go — go — go away from here!
On the other side the world he's overdue.
'Send your road is clear before you when the old
Spring-fret comes o'er you,
And the Red Gods call for you!

ON THE TWENTY-EIGHTH OF MAY, 1913, I received my appointment as surgeon to the Crocker Land Expedition to the North Polar Regions from the Committee in Charge at the American Museum of Natural History.

So for one the wet sail arching through the rainbow round the bow,
And for one the creak of snow-shoes on the crust

The main purpose of the expedition was to find and map a land Peary claimed to have seen from afar, mountains rising from the Polar Sea, northwest of Ellesmere Land, in the largest unexplored region of the world. He had named this unknown land Crocker Land. We also hoped to explore northern Greenland and Ellesmere Land more thoroughly than had been done before and to search for other lands to the west and north. Wherever man had not yet gone we wanted to go, as far as circumstances might permit. We had a host of projects in other scientific fields, including geology, zoology, botany, and ethnology.

The expedition was led by Donald B. MacMillan. The other members were Maurice C. Tanquary (Tank), Jerome Lee Allen (Allen), Jonathan Cook Small (Jot), Fitzhugh Green (Fitz), W. Elmer Ekblaw (Ek), and my airedale, Norse.

I gave an interview to the Bangor *Daily Commercial:*

> We expect to arrive at Etah, North Greenland, the northernmost Eskimo settlement, and therefore the northernmost human habitation, on August tenth. We will stay there just long enough to select from the 150

Eskimos of that area ten families of dog drivers and a large number of dogs to accompany us on the two years' trip. We will sail for Ellesmere Land, cross Flagler Bay, and establish our headquarters in that territory, building a wooden house, which will be our base for two years. Then a relief ship will bring us home.

From the time we arrive, until February first, the Arctic night will prevail, and we cannot make long excursions from our house, being limited to the two weeks of moonlight each month, when it is bright enough out of doors to read. We can make short expeditions, arranging for supplies, but it will be necessary to wait for the Arctic dawn before we can set out on our trip to Crocker Land. Once there we will split into three parties, one going north, one south, and the third directly inland. If we fail to find limits to Crocker Land in the time allowed, we will return and try again the second year. Nothing is known definitely about Crocker Land; one of the mountain peaks was seen from Cape Thomas Hubbard by Peary in 1906, at a distance of 150 miles, in the great unknown area west of northern Ellesmere Land, and this is all known of it.

In Greenland and Ellesmere Land we will be east of magnetic north and so near that the compass will be sluggish, erratic, and of little use.

Our wireless outfit will keep in touch with wireless at the Canadian military post, Wolstenholme, on Hudson Straits, and this wireless will relay messages to the Canadian station at Ottawa, which will furnish Washington authorities with all information received.

"What sort of surgical treatment do you most expect to give your party?"

Frost bites and accidents will be the most common. Colds and similar troubles that bother so much here in winter are unknown in Arctic regions, probably because of lack of dust and germs in the atmosphere. All members of the party are vaccinated for diphtheria and typhoid fever.

As it turned out, we had to establish our headquarters at Etah, North Greenland, since the ship failed to buck the ice across to Ellesmere Land. The wireless was insufficiently powerful to make any contact with the outside world. The "colds and similar troubles . . . unknown in the Arctic regions" bothered terribly whenever isolation was broken. We found Crocker Land to have been a mirage. Many of the scientific and exploratory purposes of the expedition turned into will-o'-the-wisps because of self-seeking leadership. The two years stretched into four. I came home in an entirely unexpected manner.

What was the lure that led me to go as physician and surgeon on the Crocker Land Expedition? What was the lure for me, Hal Hunt, with a medical practice in Island Falls, where I was the only doctor in a large area of rural Maine? Why did I sell my house, equipment, horse, buggy, and sleigh, and go against the wishes of my father? Why did I leave my wife, Marion, and four-year-old daughter, Ruth, with no home of their own and only the seventy-five dollars a month that was to be my pay for them to live on?

I had the ideal combination of medical training, strength, stamina, and youth to fill the position. To be worth my salt should I not go? So I thought. But, you ask, what is so important about an expedition to the North Polar

Regions? If enlarging man's knowledge is important, then, I felt, this expedition should be important, for such was its purpose.

In ancient times, everything that lay beyond the circle of familiar experience was a land of fancy. Into this realm man has penetrated gradually, and little by little, with arduous but eager labor, over mountains, forests, and tundra, has forced his way to the shores of the Arctic Ocean.

Turning to ancient history, we find that Pythias, a Greek in about the year 400 BC, was the first to report having seen the midnight sun from a point in the Thule of that time, Norway. The spherical form of the earth was conjectured then but was rejected when Christian teachings came in vogue after the fall of Rome, not to be reestablished again until the Middle Ages. In the eighth century, Iceland was discovered by the Irish, who were later driven out by the Vikings. These records mention that the sun at midnight in summer is light enough to enable one to pick lice from a shirt. I can swear to that fact, myself. About the tenth century, the Vikings visited Greenland, as far north as Upernavik. Eskimos were there before them for at least a thousand years. Gradually English, Italian, Norwegian, and American explorers penetrated farther north, until Peary reached the Pole in 1909.

There yet existed, however, north of Canada and of eastern Siberia, an area of virgin territory, some 1,500 miles in diameter, which was the largest unexplored area on the earth's surface — unowned, uninhabited, dangerous, mysterious. To penetrate one edge of this and to find the land Peary reported he had seen far out on the Polar Sea westward from Axel Heiberg Land, the Crocker Land Expedition had been outfitted. Would we be resolute enough to follow such men as Davis, Baffin, Hudson, Nansen, and Franklin, and the first men to reach the North Pole: Peary, Henson, Ootah, Egingwa, Sigloo, and Ooqueea?

To be honest with myself, the lure was adventure, albeit adventure with a purpose.

[Letter to Hal's father, Walter Lowrie Hunt, MD, of Bangor, Maine, from his uncle, Leigh R. Hunt:]

CORNING, NEW YORK
June 10, 1913

Dear Lowrie:

I am sending by this mail a bit from our local paper, which asked me about Hal's part in the Crocker Land Trip.

You must not forget that the Dutch stock has ever been inquisitive about the views just over the hill or around the corner. You want to try the next pool for trout, even if you already have a fair string of them. Even now you walk six miles through the woods, sleep outdoors without cover, tramp eighteen miles trouting the brook, and go to bed only "awfully tired." And you are sixty-four years old, and seventy years wise. Hal is old enough to feel the call of the wild, half your age, and half the rest. But the world grows by tempting fate; you do it in surgery and medicine; I have done it in education; and both prospered. There will be failures; you and I have made them, so will others; but the successes outnumber the crookednesses, and even if the individual drops out, the type moves forward immutable.

This is not saying that I should have taken the fly offered Hal, but I can see the tickling beauty of it, and sense the foretaste, and begin to look muscles and nerves over to see if I could stand the stress. The Beckers [Hal's grandmother and family] went north to the wilderness [upper New York State] under harder conditions than those under which Hal enters the Arctic. Where Hal goes, there is more help in case of need, less chance of sickness, and no more fatal results likely in case of accident. Yes, there is something in the willingness to dare that warms me clear through. I have no fears that Hal will do his part grudgingly; he will hang on till the end, and smile that quiet smile you have come to know so well. There is the same Dutch grit that built all Saxendom; you and I have been a part of it, and are not ashamed.

Some years ago I remarked at our alumni meeting that if there were one gift for me to obtain by the asking, it would be this spirit of youth for my first choice; the spirit that dares and fails and dares again till one has won out or goes down.

Yes, you will say that I have had no sons — more is the pity. But the growing loneliness of it is partly overlaid by the joy in seeing your three fruiting so well. They are valuable in suggesting what might have been.

I confess that my mind is most on what will come after. Will the associations at the New York Museum lead to some dispensation there? Will the Arctic experience help in starting again "the common task, the trivial round?" Or does the call of the wild never lessen its temperature? It is a fever in the Hunt blood, in the Becker blood. If he should have to travel awhile on an empty stomach, why, you and I have done that, and kept a steady heart, and firm mouth.

If you grow lonely with time, you still have two children; I have none. And I can see no lack of respect or love on Hal's part; it is human nature "to bear, to rear, and then to part." Every plant in the kingdom has some means whereby it flings its seeds away from the parent habitation. Nature, with a big N, evidently thought this a good plan; and if true for plants why not for animals?

You remember when you sent Hal to medical school he said he intended to use such training the best he could as long as he lived. Right or wrong, he sees the position as expedition doctor as an opportunity for this service to which he feels committed.

When you feel life stirring why not rejoice?

"Unto each the voice and vision: unto each his spoor and sign —
Lonely mountain in the Northland, misty sweat-bath
'neath the Line —
And to each a man that knows his naked soul."

Sincerely,
Rich

II

New York City to Etah, North Greenland

BY THE MIDDLE of June, I had wound up my affairs, had accepted the gift of a Sponson canoe for the expedition from my old friend, Sam Gray, of the Old Town Canoe Company, and was in New York collecting, packing, and loading on the *Diana* the medical supplies I would need.

The members of the expedition set to with a will, loading the boat to the gunwales with crate after crate. We had to take everything we might need for two years or more. Even brooms. We sweated and we grew tough in the hot sun of the New York docks. It was while we were working as stevedores, hot, sweaty, and tired, on June 30th, just two days before we were due to sail, that Dr. Hovey, chairman of the expedition, brought down to the dock the contract with the museum for the members of the expedition to sign, giving them no chance to read it, as if in a great rush. I knew that Ek had read it, had not liked it, and had requested changes. Dr. Hovey had promised to make them. I said to myself: "The museum is square; the changes will have been made," and signed it on that basis. At that late date I had no real choice.

We were not given copies at that time.

When I had an opportunity to read the contract, I saw the changes had not been made. Dr. Hovey had not intended to make them. I found out that he had carefully planned the time and circumstances of the presentation of the contract. Mac had known and had protested to Dr. Hovey, but had not informed the rest of us. The contract even went so far as to provide that the individual assumed all personal risks, and that if a member died or was disabled his pay would be stopped. What would happen to Marion and Ruth if I died or was disabled in the course of duty? I told myself: "It's all right. The museum is square."

I had met Peary a few days earlier and had asked him if he was certain he had seen Crocker Land and not a mirage. His reply was insulting, as though no one had a right to question his say-so, and who did I think I was anyway. Should I have asked myself if the ideals of the expedition to which

I had pledged myself were not also a mirage, a will-o'-the-wisp? Should I have guessed that the purposes of the museum might be subordinated by certain individuals to their own glory or gain?

In any case, I did not, then.

The second day of July, 1913, was a sweltering day in New York. The crew dressed ship, and the *Diana*, an old schooner-rigged steamship, sailed for the Arctic, with the Crocker Land Expedition aboard. We followed the so-called American route toward the North Pole, up the west coast of Newfoundland, through the Straits of Belle Isle, and close to the Labrador coast.

After a couple of weeks we were off the coast of Labrador, headed for Battle Harbor. I settled down to write letters for posting there.

GULF of ST. LAWRENCE
July 15, 1913

Dear Father:

We are having a smooth passage so far. Some fog last night but clear this morning. We will make Battle Harbor tomorrow forenoon. The ship is loaded so deep the captain has to hug the shore to dodge into a harbor in case of rough weather. There is coal up to the rail, and on top of that a lot of lumber, and on everything else 950 cases of dog biscuit. The deck is not in sight; we walk on a floor of biscuit cases. We mostly sleep on deck in our sleeping bags. The furnaces use ten tons of coal daily, and the deck load will be lowered before we start across for Greenland. Last night Tanquary and Green gave us music on mandolin and guitar. Everybody seems congenial.

I was glad to put on warm underclothes, flannel shirt, leather jacket, mittens, and overcoat this morning. Also I am wearing a Navy knit cap Walter gave me. Norse feels at home and greets everyone with great enthusiasm on first seeing them in the morning. He sleeps on the floor of my cabin. We have tried him on dog biscuit, and he seems to like them.

With love,
Hal

That night was calm and clear. I was sleeping in the deckhouse when I felt the ship slide smoothly up on a rock, then thud to a halt. At daybreak we saw we were right within a stone's throw of the shore, hard and fast aground. We began at once to try to get away before rough seas broke up the ship. For three days we shoveled our deckload of coal overboard. We unloaded our cargo into fishing boats and then onto the shore. We put anchors out astern, and the *Stella Maris*, a Canadian government vessel, came and put a line on us. Finally we slipped loose from the ledge. When we were beginning to slide off, I was in the hold shoveling soft coal into a bucket, and the purser was pulling it up on deck with a winch and dumping it into the sea. He was so excited he tipped the bucket over, and that powdery soft coal came down all over me.

BATTLE HARBOR, LABRADOR
July 19, 1913

Dear Father:

We went on the rocks of the Labrador coast midnight July 15th. Came off night of 18th, after having discharged cargo around the clock.

Replaced cargo in small boats and came here to await arrival steamer *Erik* to take us north. *Erik* larger and better ship.

Our captain no good; he drinks, and has no command of crew. Entirely his fault; gave wrong course and went below to sleep.

Have seen thousands of icebergs, some very large, and there is some snow on shore. I am in good condition and fine appetite; hungry all the time, as are the others. Norse is very well. I don't dare let him ashore as dogs would eat him up.

The captain of the *Eric* is a much better man than ours, so we anticipate no further trouble. We had a rough three days and nights, and my hands are still some scarred and sore. But for calm weather would have lost the ship.

Dr. Grenfell has a hospital here, and we have all been up to use the bathtub. Tonight we go up to have a sing about the piano, at the Doctor's house.

You will hear from me from Danish ports on South Greenland next, if we stop there.

Your son,
Hal

When we got the ship off the rock we found we could navigate fairly well. We managed to sail the damaged ship first to Battle Harbor and then to St. John's, Newfoundland. There we transhipped everything to the *Erik*, a sealer. We returned to Labrador to pick up supplies left there and crossed to the Greenland coast near Upernavik. After gales, fog, and menacing icebergs, the weather cleared for our first stop in Greenland, Cape York, to take on some Eskimos and dogs.

The airedale dog, Norse, I took with us, was just one year old. He had never had a fight beneath his coat, and we took on about 50 Eskimo dogs on the steamer at Cape York. The members of the crew told me to watch him, because if he got among the Eskimo dogs, they would kill him and eat him up. I tried to take good care of him, but I was below one day and heard an awful racket up on deck. I hurried up, and there was my little dog right in the middle of a team of Eskimo dogs; they were all stretching their traces away from him just as far as they could get. His bristles were up and he was fighting. After that, my little dog could go among the Eskimo dogs as much as he pleased, and they would give him free passage. He did get in trouble once, with a bitch with puppies. He wanted to investigate in a perfectly friendly manner, but the bitch bit his nose and would not let it go. He backed away and tried to get away from her, and it was quite some time before he could. He did not have a sufficiently heavy coat to stand the weather, so he was shivering all day long. Talking it over with the other men, I thought I had better give him to one of the officers on the ship whom he had become fond of, to take back with him.

We kept on to Etah. There we found that Smith Sound, between Greenland and Ellesmere Land, was jammed from shore to shore with packed ice floes streaming down from the north. The *Erik* found no opening, so we tied up to a convenient ledge at Etah, in Foulke Fiord, Greenland, and discharged our cargo there. It was the last of August and still daylight at midnight. We worked furiously to get everything ashore before the ship became frozen in. As soon as the cargo was discharged, the ship started south with our mail, and I had to say goodbye to Norse, as our last link with the rest of the world steamed south with him aboard.

ETAH, GREENLAND
Aug. 25, 1913

My Own True Love:

This may be the last chance I will have to write you.

We went through a very severe storm coming here. All of us were sick except Jot; Tank and Ek very much so, and I gave up my berth to Tank. I did not vomit but have missed several meals. The crew are without question not to be trusted, even as lookouts forward for ice, and are no good in any emergency. This ship only last summer ran into an iceberg in clear weather and would have sunk in rough weather. The fog makes it all doubly dangerous.

We have about given up hope of making it across to the Ellesmere Land side, on account of the ice. We are to make one last attempt today. If we fail we will go into winter quarters a short distance north of here, where we have picked out a good place to land supplies easily, and a sheltered house lot, also a fine chance for the wireless to run from the top of a high cliff.

We will attempt the Crocker Land trip just the same, going across on the ice when it becomes solid in February. It will, of course, be an extra distance, but we can have plenty of dog teams and Eskimo drivers. We dare not keep the *Erik* here much longer for fear of getting her frozen in, and we must get headquarters built soon to be free to hunt for our winter supply of food. We have sixteen walrus, one seal, one bear, thirty-nine hare, and four ptarmigan, or Arctic partridge, to date. One live baby walrus is wandering about the deck now.

I am more than homesick to see you, dear, and just to think of two years ahead yet. Will it ever come, sweetheart, when we shall be together again? I do hope you will be happy and not feel like an outcast without any home of your own to go to, having to live with relatives and friends, and teaching for a living. Last night I slept in my sleeping bag on the ground, the first one to sleep on shore.

I love you more than everything else in this world. I always shall be true to you whether you are dead or alive, and if we do not meet again in this life, please don't forget me, as I shall not you. Take care of yourself and Ruth.

Your husband,
Hal Hunt

III

Etah

> Do you know the world's white roof tree — do you know that windy rift
> Where the baffling mountain-eddies chop and change?

ETAH IS 150 miles or more north of the present Thule Air Force base. It is on Foulke Fiord, which gives on Smith Sound. In winter the sound becomes a road to Ellesmere Land, as the floe ice freezes into a solid though extraordinarily rough bridge from shore to shore north of Etah. At Etah a wicked wind funnels down the fiord from the icecap. It seems never to stop, but proximity to open water off Cape Alexander was to keep the temperature above a minus 40 degrees Fahrenheit for two years. I remember that later on at Umanak on Christmas day, 1915, with no open water around, it was 50 below, and while coming south on Christmas day, 1916, across the Melville Bay ice, our poor-quality kerosene froze at about 63 below.

The departure of the *Erik* on August 30, 1913, left us ashore on Provision Point, with our provisions and our lumber. Up the fiord was the Eskimo village of Etah, consisting of five permanent huts of sod and stone built against the hillside, and 19 men, women, and children living in their summer skin tents, or *tupiks*.

North there was no one. Anoritok, a day's journey north, showed signs of having been previously inhabited, and while we were at Etah a few of our Eskimo families tried to live there, but starvation set in and forced them south again. South of Etah was a line of tiny settlements, some at times inhabited by one family only, but totaling some 260 Eskimos, and stretching all the way to Cape York, at the northern end of Melville Bay: Sulwuddy, 20 miles south; Peteravik, 40 miles; Nerky, 50 miles; Igloodahouny, Kangerdlookswa, Keato, Kanak, Ittiboo, Umanak on North Star Bay, beside the present Air Force base, 150 miles south; Kangarsuit, Akbat in Parker Snow Bay, and the colony at Cape York, 100 miles south of Umanak. One figured distances along the most usual routes, and pretty much by guesswork. Distance was really a question of traveling conditions, as determined by the weather. When traveling was possible, there was much coming and going in search of game.

At Etah we lived in tents and started at once to build our house, Borup Lodge, about half a mile from our landing place, which became our storehouse. We had been fortunate in finding Provision Point, a cliff where it was possible to tie our vessel to the land and hold her there, with anchors out to sea, while we unloaded day and night. We had been fortunate in having a week with little wind, since usually the wind blew furiously down from the glacier.

I was designated cook. I had three meals a day for the men, and when I had a little extra time, I went hunting for Arctic rabbits. I could usually shoot a few every day; the men liked them very much indeed. Otherwise the food would be canned goods: pea soup, oatmeal, baked beans, coffee, and crackers. Meantime the house went up rapidly. We had only one carpenter, Jot, but the men did remarkably well. They learned how to drive nails and to saw boards. We tried to make foundations but could not dig into the land; it was frozen solid. We even tried dynamite. We put our foundations right on the soil itself, and it proved to be sufficiently solid to last all four years.

To add to the native population of Etah, we had brought with us from Cape York three Eskimo families: men, women, children, and their dogs. They lived in tents and were building rock igloos while we were building our house. By winter they were in their igloos and were warm. When we had finished each meal, the Eskimos could come and have what food was left. Besides that, we cooked meat especially for them. During most of the time at Etah, we ate walrus meat. It is so tasty that you can eat it day after day and still relish it, but it is tougher than any beef I ever ate in my life. We had other meat occasionally, but mostly it was that extremely tough walrus meat.

For boats we had a New Bedford whaleboat, a Swampscott dory, a flattie, a motorboat, and an Old Town Sponson canoe. The Eskimos had three kayaks. Just as soon as we could, we went hunting walrus with six oarsmen in the whaleboat and the three kayaks. When we saw walrus, the kayaks were sent ahead to harpoon the animal and put a line on him, with a float and a drag. Harpooned, the walrus always dove. When he came up for air we shot him in the head, killed him, and pulled him in on the harpoon line. When we were offshore hunting walrus and had killed two or three, we would tie them to the motorboat and drag them into the harbor, strand them out at high tide, and cut them up. By the time the harbor was frozen over, we had about 20 walrus for winter food for man and dog.

We got many eider ducks and their eggs; we figured we had about 5,000 eggs at one time, but I think that was an exaggeration. The ducks nest on an island about ten miles north of Etah, and at that time of year the young were beginning to fly. We shot all we could and put them away in storage for winter use.

At the head of the harbor was a strip of land about 200 yards wide, then a little lake, a few acres in extent, and beyond that Brother John's Glacier, which came down from the icecap. A stream flowed from the lake to salt water. Jot made a net, which we put in the stream, where we caught a few sea trout. We did not catch any fish in the sea, and as far as we know, no one north of Cape York caught any saltwater fish, except a few inedible basking sharks.

Later, about the last of October, the harbor froze over. From then on the fiord was covered with thick saltwater ice and we had little to do at Etah. During that time I again hunted rabbits every day, to store for the winter. The rabbits were much larger than those in Maine, weighing probably seven or eight pounds. The Eskimos used the skins for stockings. I used to go off alone hunting, and the men were worried about my breaking a leg or something and not getting back, so they decided that I must have an Eskimo with me. That worked out all right for a few days, but the Eskimo got tired of it and would not go, so I continued to hunt alone.

As soon as the house was finished, my job as cook ended, and the real cook, Jot, took over. He made better bread than I have ever had at home. We tried to have our meat rare to prevent scurvy. Since we had plenty of eggs, we could make cake, and I remember one day I made a first-rate sponge cake. I put it in the pantry, thinking I would bring it out at dinner as a surprise; at dinnertime I went to look at it, and it was all gone. I still don't know who ate it. When the Eskimos came in for breakfast, we gave them oatmeal and molasses. Jot was liberal with the molasses, and the Eskimos did not like so much sweet, but for a people who had not had any carbohydrates for generations, they did very well on oatmeal.

Our goods lay all over the place all the time. Of course we had many things that the Eskimos liked and needed: knives, guns, powder, shot. Their game was always very fat, and they liked a long-bladed knife to keep their hands out of the fat. We had many of those long-bladed butcher knives, which were also fine for cutting snow blocks for snow houses. The Eskimos never took anything, except one boy who took a jackknife. His mother made him bring it back, and he gave it up tearfully.

This cook of ours, Jot Small, was a character worth talking about. He was from an old-style Provincetown family. He was good at everything, but he had almost no education; he found it difficult to write his own name. He was a skilled carpenter, a fair cook, a first-class boatbuilder, and a good mechanic for the boat engine. Jot was the only uneducated man in our party, but he put the other men right back where they belonged. He was splendid in an argument; he had them all licked. His language was old-style Provincetown, and the others didn't like it very much, but he said, "Language is what you make it." He would take either side of a question. He would argue on one side for maybe two or three days and then would argue directly on the other side.

At Etah the partitions between the bunk rooms were single boards, and the cracks were wide. Next to Jot's bunk, in the adjoining room, was Allen, who complained continually about being "so awful lousy." Jot finally told him, "I've been poking lice through the cracks in our partition, and that's where you got all your lice."

I helped Jot make a kayak for himself. It was different from the Eskimo kayaks, although it had a wood framework covered with sealskin, as did theirs. He was going out hunting walrus in it, so we fitted him out with everything: paddle, harpoon, sealskin float, line, and drag. We went out with the whaleboat where the walrus were, put him out on the sea in his kayak, and showed him the walrus. He paddled up to the walrus, turned around, and came back again. He told us that the nearer he got to the walrus the bigger that walrus seemed, and "If you don't look out for yourself, no one will."

When the wind blew so hard we could not use boats, we had to tote whatever we needed the half mile from Provision Point. That included bags of soft coal, bags of flour, and boxes of crackers, dog food, and canned goods. Some of the men became quite proficient at carrying big packs on a tump line and vied to see how heavy a load they could carry. I know Ek and Tank could each carry 125 pounds.

Mac had a room to himself, and the rest of us had double rooms. We had no skins at that time, only army blankets. I think I had 16 on my bunk, part of them over me and part underneath. I was rooming with Allen, the Navy electrician, an extremely nice fellow. He had been recently married and was a mighty homesick man. He was to put up the wireless, and to receive and send, and he did a wonderful job, but neither was possible. He set up a generator, and we had electricity all the time.

We were intent on making the house warm enough. It was built well. On the front and two sides was a covered porch where we could store provisions. That shed had windows, and the house had double windows. They were stuffed tightly with oakum so there was no draft, and between the double windows was about six inches of rocksalt to take up the moisture. That did so well that even in the coldest days of winter the windows did not frost over; we could see out plainly. The stove was in the middle of the room, with the pantry directly behind it. Anyone who wanted a lunch could get what he wanted at any time, as long as he did not get in the way of the cook. We all learned to cook, because one man was always on duty, day and night, and he was often hungry. He watched the instrument panel and logged temperature, barometric pressure, and wind speed. Our stove was an ordinary Crawford cooking range, and we were burning soft coal, so soft it was just like flour. We had to learn how to use it, and we finally did. When stoking the stove with soft coal, one got a shovelful of coal ready, opened all the drafts, lifted a cover, shoved in the coal, and put the cover down at once, quickly, to keep coal smoke from coming into the room. It was not possible to do a very good job, and soon the ceiling of the house was just as black as the coal, but even on the coldest days the stove kept the house warm enough. The draft was good because of the difference in temperature between indoors and outdoors.

The nearest white men, the only ones for over 1,000 miles, were 150 miles south, at Umanak, where Knud Rasmussen and Peter Freuchen kept a trading post, swapping sledge runners, knives, needles, guns, ammunition, cloth, and tobacco for furs. Two wooden houses were there: the two-room trading post and a mission house, the latter usually empty. We rented it part of the time. Knud and Peter visited us at Etah off and on, and I stayed with

Peter and in the mission house much of the time from the fall of 1915 to the late summer of 1916.

Knud's father was Danish and his mother a Greenlander. He had spent his childhood in South Greenland. He was the senior partner and leader of the post. He had a thorough knowledge and understanding of the Eskimos, and he cared deeply about their welfare. His natural leadership and authority was recognized by all the North Greenland Eskimos. He knew every one of those Polar Eskimos, their history, beliefs, and folk tales. He wrote a remarkable book about his first year spent among them in 1903-1904, called in its English translation *People of the Polar North* (London, 1908).

Rasmussen was, however, careless in travel. When we crossed Melville Bay in December, 1916, he allowed only three days' provisions; it took us ten days. He took only skis and found he could not use them in the rough going, whereas he had teased that I would not be able to keep up with him. I led the whole way on my snowshoes. He took whisky along. He put some in my tea, which spoiled the tea. He had women on the trip, and that slowed us down.

Peter and Knud never desired to make more than a living. They were ambitious to visit all the Eskimo tribes and villages from Greenland across Baffin Land and Canada to Alaska; they wanted to study all the folklore and customs of the different tribes, an excellent project. They asked me to go with them, but even had I been free to do so, I would not have gone, because they were poor planners. They started out with too many people, too little food, and the wrong kind of equipment.

I saw a lot of Peter, who was unlike anyone I had ever known. He was a socialist, and he believed in free love. He was an interesting talker, if not always credible. I heard that he told people how he knocked out, with a hammer, the front teeth of an Eskimo who could not open his mouth to eat. In truth it was I who pulled them out with forceps.

Peter and his Eskimo wife, Navarana, lived much in the Eskimo way. I was with them when she had her first baby. There was a party on. Navarana said: "You will have to excuse me for a moment," and she went out. After what seemed to me like fifteen minutes she came back and told Peter: "Well, it didn't hurt half as much as they said it would." Peter said: "What didn't hurt?" "Having the baby."

I went to examine the baby, and he was a tiny dark thing, about four pounds, but seemed healthy. He looked wholly Eskimo, and I think he was. The second child was Peter's.

Peter and Knud were likeable men. They quite rightly felt that Mac had no business to trade for fox skins and were angry, as was I, that Dr. Hovey kept for himself the tobacco Peter had supplied for the whole crew of the *Cluett*. In spite of this, Knud and Peter continued to cooperate with the expedition all the way.

Early in 1914 Peter and I went together across to Ellesmere Land to take supplies for Mac's Crocker Land trip. We stayed for a while at what was left of the old wooden hut on Pim Island that Peary had used as headquarters for his attempt at the North Pole in 1900. Traveling Eskimos had torn out the floor and a partition for the wood, so we worked on it several days and fixed it up as well as we could. Peter was a good companion, but one could not depend on him. The Eskimos knew this and told me, so I took care. Tank and Ek learned it early on. Peter invited them to sledge to Umanak with him in April, 1914, to return to Etah when open water would allow the use of a powerboat. He persuaded them that he lived in a land of plenty and that it would all be theirs. When Mac fetched them in August, they were thin, hungry, worried, and mighty glad to come home to Etah.

Fundamentally the Danes did not look with favor on American explorers who traded for furs that they thought should have been theirs, yet they were friendly and helpful. They certainly enjoyed having company and liked the opportunity to improve their English. Peter had a great admiration for Knud, and used to say, "Knud is a whole man; I am only half a man." It was Knud who renamed Umanak, Thule, not pronouncing the final *e*. (That is how the present American Air Force Base got its name. The Eskimo village of Thule has been moved north, to the settlement of Kanak.)

So we settled in at Etah, seven white men in very close quarters, surrounded by friendly brown faces, and with Knud Rasmussen and Peter Freuchen at Umanak.

IV

The Polar Inuit, 1913-1917

NOW IS THE TIME to tell you about those friendly brown faces that surrounded me for years, and to whom I was *Nagorsakswa*, big doctor, or *Nanooksw*a, big bear, because, they said, my big feet made tracks in the snow like a polar bear's.

Among them were the Eskimos who went to the Pole with Peary: prosperous wise old Ootah, strong Egingwa, with the clean wife, uncomplaining Sigloo, for whom I traveled many miles to amputate his foot, and lame, plucky little Ooqueea. Ooqueea and one other Eskimo, Akpoodashaho, became as close to me as my own brother, perhaps closer. Before I continue the account of my experiences, you should know them, how they lived, and how they watched over us and taught us the skills we needed to survive.

Eskimos call themselves simply *Inuit*, their word for people. They live all along the Arctic coast of North America, including Alaska and Labrador, the Arctic Islands, and Greenland; their refuse heaps seem to show an existence there for 2,000 years or more. The 19 Inuit we found at Etah formed the northernmost settlement of the entire world, living literally on the edge of human existence. They still do. They are part of the North Greenland or Polar Eskimo tribe, also referred to as the Cape York or Smith Sound Eskimos, since they are nomads, scattered all along that coast, to be found wherever game is most plentiful. The vast expanse of Melville Bay separates them from South Greenland Inuit and Greenlanders (part Eskimo and part white), and communication between them is limited.

Theirs is still a true stone-age culture, little modified by the steel and matches that white explorers and traders have given them, just enough to raise their standard of living above subsistence level. Their tribal stories tell of starvation causing suicide, infanticide, murder, and cannibalism in ancient times. One of the older men, Panikpa, told us of his grandfather's coming with his tribe across Smith Sound from Ellesmere Land, and before that from Baffin Land. They found in North Greenland a few very primitive Inuit, at Etah or Anoritok. His ancestors introduced or reintroduced the *umiak*, the kayak, and the bow and arrow to the tribe. This must have been about the middle of the last century.

These Polar Inuit are a cheerful, happy lot, joking and laughing all the time. They are brave, faithful, and sunny-tempered, showing devotion to children and old people. They are also extremely honest in all dealings. Their only means of doing business is bartering in furs. They are always friendly, and because they have little contact with the outside world, they believe everything that is told them, placing great faith in white men. In some ways they are so simple-minded as to be like small children, and yet in others they are astute. They can size up their visitors with a keen directness that many might envy. They considered Dr. Cook a charlatan from the very first, but looked upon Peary as a genuine leader immediately. They enjoyed our companionship as well as the material goods we could provide, and they were always eager to go on trips with us.

The Eskimos who came to Borup Lodge had table manners, in their own way. Usually more careful than us not to be the first to eat, they shared and shared alike the big kettle of meat we cooked for them. Instead of sitting on the floor, as would be normal for them, they sat at our table. I remember one exception among these well-mannered people. Nookapingwa was a young man spoiled by an old mother. He would take all the hunks of pineapple and wolf them down, unchewed. One time his wife, Wewe, came to me: "Nookapingwa has a pain in his belly and wants you to come to him in his igloo. Too much pineapple." He also once started to sample a bottle of whisky we had out for a birthday party. Soon there was an empty bottle and a royally drunk Nookapingwa.

Eskimos have a tremendous sense of fun; igloos and tupiks are filled with the sound of laughing and giggling. They play football with a walrus bladder on moonlit nights, the members of the whole village screaming and kicking the football. We taught them baseball, and they bent over with laughter when they caught a fly ball. They like cards but can count only to twenty, although some children are learning to read and write from the missionaries. I taught chess to one Eskimo, and his skill amazed everyone.

Eskimos are expert carvers and make all kinds of small figures and ivory toys for the children. They made a fish that seems to swim, hanging on strings like a puppet, for me to take home to my little girl. Inventive, deft, and showing unusual mechanical ability, they can take apart and put together again an automatic rifle the first time they've ever seen one.

The Polar Inuit are the most unusual people, perhaps, in the world. They have no religion in our sense of the word, no government, no tribal leaders, no marriage rites. They are mutually considerate and live by a code that is clean and foursquare, sharing freely with one another all that they have: food, clothing, and even a wife. They live a completely communal existence. When an Eskimo does not do his share of the work, no resentment is harbored against him. The other Eskimos pity him, give him an equal share of the food, build him an igloo, and find him a wife, even though they scorn him.

Generous and hospitable, they will share the last bit of meat with a stranger. If you go into an igloo and like the occupant, you immediately take a piece of meat and eat it, either raw or from the pot, and then those in the igloo know you for a friend. You are not asked to take it, but you are watched to see if you do or not. When you have, they say: "That is very nice."

Ptarmigan should have been plentiful, but were not so around Etah. In the spring there would be a few, and I remember one year Akpoodashaho brought me the first one of the season, a delicacy to him and to me. I did not dare refuse it, because an Eskimo is offended if you do. I ate it, picked the bones carefully — the Eskimo wastes nothing — and tossed the carcass to a dog. Akpoodashaho grabbed that dog, choked him, retrieved the mass of bones, and after chewing off every shred until the bones shone, he tossed it back to the hungry-eyed dog.

They also share that which white people are wont to cherish and keep for themselves. They do it in an open, aboveboard manner that is seldom seen in more civilized countries. Often, as is the custom, my host has offered me his wife. They had a hard time understanding my refusal. "*Nanookswa* must be very tired," or "He must be very much in love." I did not tell them how little Eskimo women attracted me. Eskimos smell. They smell something awful.

They never fight or speak crossly, very seldom strike another person. I know just one man who beat his wife, and finally she turned on him and gave him a licking, and he never did it again. The children are utterly spoiled. They are never punished and can have just what they want. I have seen a child come up and take the candy his parent was eating. I never saw an Eskimo strike a child the four years I was there. The children are, nonetheless, unusually pleasant, reasonable, and well-mannered, and grow up to be fine, able men and women while still teenagers. Continually sharing the life of their parents prepares them to wrest a living from their environment. Each boy longs to be a great hunter and each girl longs to catch foxes and make a fine jacket of them, so in their play they learn these skills.

A young man and woman attracted to each other simply form a partnership that continues as long as it is mutually agreeable, and such partnerships are broken less frequently than formal marriages of civilized peoples. If the wife accepts the love of another member of the tribe, it is considered quite proper and in good form as long as the husband is told of it. He will offer no objection. Failure to tell him, however, is considered a breach of etiquette.

The men in our party were very decent about the Eskimo women, although they did not all feel as I did. One of the men told me that, when he had asked to sleep with one woman, she said, "No, it is taught us that two men are enough for one woman and I have my husband and Mr. Mac." Peary had his regular Eskimo wife who bore him two sons. She said: "When I was Peary's wife I was with no one else." When Peary was last north, he took a younger woman with him on his trip, but when he returned he went off in the hills with his former wife, and the result was the second son.

The women are modest, in their way, never making advances, but when a white man makes an advance he is gladly met half way. Immoral?

Say rather unmoral, an altogether different thing. Look at this in its broader aspect, and you will see that immorality and sin, as the white people understand them, have not yet touched the Polar Inuit. But let the white men come in any numbers, let religion be introduced clumsily and tactlessly, and the whole tribe would reek with sin.

If Christ should appear among the Polar Inuit today, I doubt if conditions would be greatly changed by His coming. He would find there the same lack of selfishness, jealousy, and unkindness that He has taught.

While they have no formal religion, the Polar Inuit do believe they will live again. The spirit will still live. A newborn baby is named after a person who has died, and the spirit of that person comes to the child. If a man names his son after the grandfather, the father becomes the son, and the child calls his own father, son. This may partly explain the great consideration shown to children and old people.

Torngak, the devil, lives up on the icecap, but it seems to me that they do not fear him, that it is not a personal matter but more like folklore. The Eskimos do not seem to have any ideas of God or a great spirit. Everything outside the everyday is caused by an impersonal force that permeates existence. It just is. They do not attempt to explain lightning or storms, saying that is the way things are. They are not impressed by the telephone, considering it merely another unexplained phenomenon.

The stars in the sky, the sun and the moon, all have names and stories associated with them, just as among other peoples. The Big Dipper, for example, is a herd of caribou. Because my language was limited, I could not understand the tales that the Inuit related to each other with great vivacity, but I could not see that their daily lives and hunting trips were much more affected by superstition than are ours.

The Polar Inuit accepted my medical techniques and the use of ether and pills without question. I was an *angekok,* a medicine man, a person with special skills, possibly magical, certainly beyond their understanding. As far as I know, I was the only medicine man at that time, although they existed in recent tribal tradition.

Eskimo clothing is perfectly adapted to their environment. If we were to bring an Inuit to Maine and dress him as we dress, he would freeze to death on a cold winter day. The women made us all complete outfits before the first winter set in. While dressed in their fur clothing, one does not feel the cold unless a bad storm is raging. Then the wind bullies its way through the toughest of clothing, and the noses and cheeks of native and white man alike will be frostbitten. In the late winter and in the spring, snow goggles are indispensable. As a rule, the Inuit make them of wood with a narrow slit to see through. Some of our men were not careful to use dark glasses and suffered intensely as a result.

In the summer sun, out of the wind, an Eskimo baby will play on a fur skin quite naked, warm, and happy to be free of clothes. The women will sit sewing or nursing their babies outside their *tupiks,* as they do also in their winter igloos, wearing only their little foxskin panties. The ever-circling sun brings forth grasses, moss, and tiny flowers hiding among the rocks of the seemingly barren land. It also brings forth swarms of immense, voracious mosquitoes, against which we had no defense.

The Polar Inuit wears a shirt of beautifully patterned birdskins with the feathers inside, then a hooded jacket, or *kooletah*, often of caribou, and mittens, usually of sealskin. Over underpants and stockings of rabbit go bearskin pants with bearskin or sealskin boots: *kamiks* or *mukluks*. Boot soles are made from the very tough hide of the big bearded seal, less common than the smaller ringed seal. Between stockings and boots, one puts a layer of a fine grass, to be found only in certain places. A bag of this grass is carried on all trips; it absorbs moisture, so it is changed every day. The bag also serves as a pillow. The grass is gathered in the summer, and until otherwise needed, is used to pad the sleeping platform. I found that a fine grade of excelsior served about as well.

When I first arrived and traveled with the Eskimos, they carefully lined my *kamiks* with the grass, but when they found I would do it myself, they paid no more attention. One of our men, Ekblaw, was careless about it, and sometimes frosted the bottoms of his feet slightly. Even with a dog team and smooth going, one must walk a little to keep one's feet warm. If feet get chilly, one gets frostbite, and one man who was careless froze both big toes. He knew they were frozen, and he told me he had not taken off his *kamiks* for five days. So we took them off, and sure enough, both toes were frozen. Then we had to wait to see the line of demarcation between frozen and healthy tissue. When that happened, we gave him ether and took off his big toes.

Babies, bare-bottomed, wear a hooded jacket and are carried everywhere on their mothers' backs, in a special hood, or rather an enlargement of the *kooletah*. The mothers seem very skillful at swiftly pulling the babies out at just the right moment.

The women chew all the skins to be used for clothing to make them sufficiently pliable. Their teeth wear right down to the gums, but they never have a toothache. They make their own thread of sinews from the backs of whales, walrus, and caribou, and, before we brought needles, they made their own from ivory and bone. The sinew seemed to me superior to what was being used at that time for surgical sutures. I brought some home but then did nothing about it, which was a mistake.

The Polar Inuit's permanent winter igloo is built up with stones and sod on the sides and roofed over with whatever they can find, usually flat stones topped with sod. To let in some light, an igloo has a window made of the bearded seal's intestines, with a tiny peephole for looking out. One enters through a low tunnel perhaps ten feet long. The house has three levels up to the bed and living platform. An igloo is always too hot. One takes off one's jacket, bare to the skin, and if one dares, one also takes off one's pants. Baths? An Eskimo gets one bath in his life: when he is born, his mother licks him clean and dry. Eskimos believe a good strong smell keeps Torngak away. There is a urine pot in the igloo, but there is no outhouse, and, believe me, you bring a bare bottom in through that tunnel pretty fast, especially if there is a dog outside.

The summer house is the *tupik*, a tent of carefully sewn sealskins, held up by poles and down by a ring of very heavy stones. It is strong and will withstand rain, snow, and gale-force winds. The Inuit take the cover off the winter igloo so it will air and dry out. Early in September, they clean it out, thoroughly cover it again, and make it airtight for the coming winter.

The Eskimo wife seems to have the say as to where they shall live. She tells her husband: "We've been here long enough and must go elsewhere for the next year." It is not difficult for them to move, as all belongings, often not much more than furs, weapons and a stove, can be put on one sled.

The Polar Inuit is a skilled architect. The stone and sod igloo, his permanent home, is built on the cantilever principle. It is primitive only for the lack of proper building materials.

The snow igloo is a dome; the blocks are cut and then built up in a spiral, in such a way that they support each other by mutual pressure, the whole held together by the keystone. It takes a good man to build one, even a small one, about five feet by eight, built just for the night. When one is traveling, toward the end of the day the Eskimo begins to feel the snow with his knife, to locate a snow bank hard enough, well packed by the wind, to cut into blocks about two feet by three. One man works outside and one inside. A low igloo is warmer but more difficult to make than one with a high dome. If the Eskimo intends to stay a few weeks, he will build a bigger igloo with an entrance tunnel and heat it up until snow melts on the inside to form a coating of solid ice when it cools. A hole in the top lets out heat and smoke. At night he sticks his mitten into the hole and blocks the doorway with a hunk of snow. Often, if he is going to stay there some time, a good man will line this bigger snow house with skins. He leaves a space between the ice lining and the skins. To hold up the skin lining, he attaches thongs, which he passes through the igloo walls and secures with bits of bone on the outside. These igloos are very warm and will last all winter.

Clothes are often left outside or in a type of entrance hall. This gives one more freedom to move, airs the clothes, and kills the body lice, with which all Polar Inuit are afflicted. When the louse is cold, he just curls up his legs and drops off. White men have somewhat changed this good custom of nakedness. When fur clothes are taken indoors, they must first be beaten with a *tilugtut*, a round-edged, sword-shaped snow beater, to remove the snow, as it is essential that clothes be kept dry.

I tried once in Maine to make a snow house when I thought the snow was packed hard enough by the wind. I got the sides all right, but the snow was too soft and wouldn't hold when I tried to lean the blocks in to form the dome. I never was very good at it anyway.

The top platform of a North Greenland home is at the back and covered with furs. Usually there are two lamps on a lower level, one on each side of the entrance. They serve for cooking, heating, and lighting. It is this blubber lamp, or *ikama*, that has made Eskimos independent of firewood, and thus made it possible for them to exist so far north. The *ikama*, which is both lamp and stove, is a shallow soapstone saucer about three feet long. In a pinch one can substitute an old frypan. Along the edge they place a dam of a special type of ground-up moss, and in the center a piece of blubber, just touching the moss. Twirling a bow drill, they work up enough friction to get sparks on the moss and melt fat to start the flame. Once fire is started, oil from the blubber melts gradually, and the moss serves as a wick. Seal or walrus blubber will do, but narwhal or white whale fat is best, and such a fire, well tended, will not smoke. I found it hard to start the *ikama* even with matches, and without matches it is a long and wearisome operation for the most skilled. This is the one great difficulty in moving from place to place. Thus matches have changed the lives of the Polar Inuit more than any other tool, enabling them to move after game much more freely. If they have matches for a generation or two, they will probably forget how to make a fire with a bow drill. The only kitchen utensil a woman has is a rough knife, shaped like our chopping knife, which she uses to scrape hair off skins, cut the skins for clothes, cut up meat for the pot, etc.

The only foods available are meat, fish, and eggs. Since the Inuit eat all parts of the animal and eat some meat raw, there is no malnutrition. I have never seen scurvy among the Polar Inuit, although I have among the South Greenlanders.

They eat their favorite tidbits as the animal is being cut up. Bits of narwhal skin or clams from the stomach of a walrus are eaten immediately. Walrus dig for clams with their tusks, crush them in their mouths, and suck out the meat. They have three stomachs. The clams in the first stomach taste just like those we eat in Maine.

If you take meat from the soapstone pot over the stove, you can use the rib of a seal. If you have raw meat, frozen or not, you put between your teeth as much as you can get in your mouth. Then you hold a knife parallel to your face and saw off the portion of the meat that you cannot swallow. Of course, you can take the end off your nose in the process, but I never had any trouble eating Eskimo fashion. At first, we did not like eating clams fresh from the stomach of a walrus, but we soon learned that they are delicious, and they are all shucked too. Eskimos also like very high meat, and they have one dish that is too much for me. They fill a sealskin bag with little auks, whole, feathers and all, surrounded with blubber, and leave it in a shady place to rot for months before enjoying the contents.

Babies, almost from the first day, are given chewed-up meat in very small pieces, and this is done also for old people.

The Eskimo dogs are descendants of wolves, tamed hundreds or thousands of years ago. For travel and hunting, they are essential to the Polar Inuit. They are by far the most wonderful and most faithful animals in the world. When dogs become tired, they must be taken from the harness and tied to the sled, or else they will take their places beside the other dogs and run until they drop dead. They are savage, not so much to man, but they attack each other or any other animal they think they can whip. The Polar Inuit keep their dogs in harness constantly, as they would run away and fight each other if let loose. The South Greenlanders let their dogs run free, which causes all kinds of trouble. To prevent the dogs from chewing the harness and gaining freedom in this manner, their back teeth are knocked out with a hatchet, a cruel and revolting, but necessary, practice.

Each team has a king dog who has become boss by licking all the others. He keeps order in that team, although a bitch in heat upsets the team no end. On the whole, Eskimos control their dogs by brutality, which is not necessary. Once when we were on a trip, a bitch in an Eskimo's team started to have puppies. They were left along the trail as the trip continued. I had a team of dogs that was affectionate, easy to handle, and performed as well as the other teams, if not better, because I made friends with them, although they knew I would stand no nonsense. A few dogs are pets, and sleep in, but these do not make good sled dogs. Sometimes one may get loose. Once a stray dog got into Borup Lodge. I chased him around and around the room, around the kitchen stove and the table in the middle, and could not catch him. Finally, with a leap, he went out headfirst through the double-glass windows, taking the windows with him, and we did not have too many left.

Greenland Eskimos hitch each dog to the sled on its own separate line, and the dogs fan out, the lead dog in the center. This way one can see that each dog pulls equally. The lines get tangled continually. The drivers have to take their mittens off to unsnarl the lines, and fingers become cold, stiff, and often frostbitten. One has to use teeth, too, and the traces are not exactly clean. An Eskimo dog whip is a long thong on a short handle, and the snap of a whip above a dog's back is like a pistol shot. A shirker leans into the harness with a will. An Eskimo can hit any part of any dog, and the dog knows it. A snap on the right and the dogs turn left, on the left and they turn right. I became quite proficient with the whip, but a beginner can wrap a thong around his own leg quite painfully.

These intelligent animals rarely will go on treacherous ice, and they have saved my life this way. Eight dogs can pull 800 pounds. They will travel 30 miles a day on one pound of pemmican each, and this is not the best food for them. Pemmican is a food made chiefly of dried meat and suet, although other ingredients are usually added to make it more palatable if it is for human consumption. We were furnished with two kinds of pemmican, one for dogs and one for ourselves.

Dogs need fresh meat to do really well, although they will pull until they drop dead in their traces, and on empty stomachs at that. I have traveled 24 hours steadily with dogs, and at another time went 100 miles on a rush call with only a few hours' rest and very little food.

The Polar Eskimos and their dogs are the best of traveling companions, but traveling with a dog team is often sheer drudgery. One nearly always walks alongside the sledge to relieve the dogs. If the trail lies across piled-up floe ice, progress is agonizingly slow. The sledge is shoved and hauled over one pressure ridge, only to plunge down the other side and tip over or bury its nose in the next one — dogs, traces, and sledge in a mess. We had to carry a pick axe to cut a way through the rough up-ended floes of the sea ice.

The Polar Inuit have for years been starved for wood to make sledges, harpoons, kayaks, and paddles. What wood they have, except for that given them by explorers, whalers, and traders, is only small pieces of driftwood, which came originally from the rivers of Siberia and drifted in the ice pack across the North Pole, down between Iceland and Greenland, and then up the west coast of Greenland to Cape York. They have to lash these small pieces of wood together with sealskin lines to make their harpoons, the frames of kayaks, etc. When we were there, they had no *umiak*, an open rowboat, what they called a "woman's" boat, only a history of having had one, from Panikpa's people.

To make a kayak, the men lash together a frame, preferably of wood, for which bone sometimes had to be substituted in the past. Women scrape the hair off about six large sealskins, then with all working together as in a sewing bee, they stretch the skin over the frame and sew it with sinew, which swells and fills the needle holes so the kayak never leaks. For paddling a kayak you wear a sealskin jacket, tight at the hood and wrists, and tied around the kayak opening, so all is watertight. Many of the North Greenland kayaks are so limber that when they are lifted to be put into the water there has to be one person on each end and one in the middle, supporting it.

Flint, which the Indians used, is not to be found in the Cape York district. As much as they can, the Inuit use Caribou horns, walrus tusks, and narwhal horn. For harpoon points, they carve sharpened pieces of caribou antlers. Occasionally they could pound off a chip from a meteorite that fell a long time ago in the southern part of their territory. This they would use as a knife blade. Sometimes a whaler came to their land, and knives were available through trade, even in the last century, so they have had knives for some time.

The coming of the white man, who brought steel, lumber, and matches, was of great benefit. Knives are important. Steel points make Eskimo harpoons much more effective, and the Inuit's principal diet is seal and walrus. Whether or not the introduction of the gun was a benefit is questionable. The Eskimos tend to overkill, and when game or ammunition runs out they will starve.

One walrus, weighing about a ton, provides food for a family and dog team for about one month. The skin, with some meat on it, is fed to the dogs. It is cut in strips so they can swallow it end on. There is no other use for this skin, which is about two inches thick, inflexible, and very tough. Sealskin is used for clothing, tents, and kayaks, and all the rest of the seal is eaten except the bones. When they can get some other meat, they prefer it, but often they have nothing else.

Greenland Eskimos are proficient in harpooning from a kayak, which is no small feat. Walrus eat everything from krill and clams to small seals, and sometimes I thought one was going to eat me. Although Inuit never seek danger and are as prudent as can be, we did lose three of our Eskimo friends while walrus hunting. One man had a walrus come up right under him and tip him over. To harpoon a walrus, two kayak men go ahead of the whaleboat, with a float and drag fastened on a line to the detachable harpoon point. The kayak man has to jab with the harpoon and paddle away fast, turning quickly to the left, away from the walrus. Then, in the *umiak* or whaleboat, others chase the walrus and put a bullet into his head when he comes up. I have shot many. Walrus swim about seven miles an hour, and we could not catch them with the whaleboat. They stay under water about eleven minutes, and we used to time them with our watch and then look to see where they would come up.

Once I was rowing stroke in the whaleboat with five Eskimo women, chasing a harpooned walrus. By custom, only women row; it is beneath the dignity of a man to use an oar. Suddenly an Eskimo said to me, laughing heartily, "Are you a woman, *Nagorsakswa?* How many babies have you had?" About that time my oar broke, the only really good oar we had left. Later one of the Eskimos took it, and with only a butcher knife, he fitted the pieces together, wrapped a sealskin line around it, and it was better than ever.

Another time we were hunting walrus and an ugly head suddenly stuck up by the rail of the whaleboat close to Etookashoo's face. They were looking eye to eye at each other. Etookashoo, terror in his face, fell off his seat into the bottom of the boat. The walrus dived.

If a man is hunting alone and gets a walrus or seal, all the kayaks in sight help with tow lines to beach the animal. Each man in the party puts his hand on a part of the animal he wants. That part will be given to him, and the harpooner gets what is left. Once, in my kayak, I shot and brought in a seal alone, and beached him. I had shot his head off. You have to be confounded accurate to shoot a swimming seal, as just the head shows a little above water, looking hardly larger than a duck. Because seals get very fat in summer, he did not sink. In my kayak, I pulled alongside till I could grab his hind flipper, got a line on it, and hauled him in that way. He was a big one, about a thousand pounds. A single Eskimo came up and said: "*Nagorsakswa,* a lot of men are coming. You better cut him up NOW."

To get seal in winter, I often crawled along to the seal's breathing hole on the ice or on a little sled, hiding behind a small, white sail. When the seal came up to breathe, I jabbed the harpoon, played him on the line like a salmon, then shot him when he came up to breathe again. I hunted walrus in winter, too. It is easy to know where they are because they stay in herds and are always bellowing to each other, winter or summer. Sometimes they sleep on the surface of the ice, and sometimes they are in leads of open water. Leads are gaps in the ice caused by wind, tide, and currents. They are common between land-fast ice and sea ice, and they may open up anywhere out to sea, as the ice everywhere is remarkably mobile. They are a danger to always look out for. The Polar Inuit must hunt the great beasts of the sea wherever they can be found, and they depend on their arrival in certain areas each winter.

In addition to seal, walrus, and narwhal, the Inuit are dependent for their livelihood on their ability to get bear, musk ox, caribou, hare, fox, birds, and eggs. It is variety of game that averts scarcity and famine. They are skilled not only with the harpoon but also with bow and arrow, snares, slingshots, stone traps, and the great long-handled nets that they make to catch little auks, eider, and other ducks that arrive in the spring by the thousands.

The oyster-sized breast of the little auk or dovekie is delicious. It tastes like pigeon, only better. There are so many in season that their dense swarms shadow the land. The women and children go after them with glee, and as they catch them, picnic on them raw until they are stuffed. What they cannot eat they store under great piles of rocks. I myself have eaten several dozen raw at one time. Their skins make the best undershirts.

Eggs of all ducks are cached under stones and eaten all year as needed. A rotten egg is not harmful, even one with a chick in it about to be hatched. We ate them, too. Wolf, narwhal, and whale are often not available. Meat is cached in the shade under a great pile of stones, even for as long as a year.

Skins have a new importance, to be traded with the white man for knives and needles, harpoon tips, wood, matches, and occasionally a gun and shot, the first tools to bring the Polar Inuit out of the stone age.

These light-hearted people live continually on the edge of starvation. One time in 1916 we ran out of food in a small settlement. An Eskimo woman begged dog biscuits from me for her children, and I gave them to her. I was glad to eat the biscuits too, not because I relished them — they were made in England of meal and horsemeat, and one could get a cud of bones and hair — but because I was working hard on a starvation diet. I can't look at dog biscuit now.

Lack of game or loss of a skilled hunter means hunger and often death to the survivors. One woman was left stranded on an island with three children when her husband drowned in his kayak. She was isolated. She knew she could not feed all three. She finally asked them if they would rather starve or be put out of their misery. Two said they would rather be put away. This meant she had to put a sealskin line around their throats and throttle them. I knew the one who said he would stick it out with his mother. Help finally came. He said he was unusually small because he had had so little to eat for so long. He was a fine hunter and a fine companion.

Only their ingenuity and skill have made it possible for the Polar Inuit to live in this inhospitable land. To exist at all, they must live constantly with danger, danger of death. So did we, for although we had far better tools for survival, we were far less skillful. We could have done nothing without the Inuit's knowledge, competence, and friendly cooperation. Equally important, we learned from them to persevere, to improvise, and to do without. The Eskimos saved Peary's life; they saved Dr. Cook's life. They saved mine time and time again; I think they saved the other men's lives, too.

They did not ask for us to come; we literally invaded their territory. They welcomed us and shared with us. We will disrupt the equilibrium of their society, and I wonder if we can in any way help them to hold onto their great qualities of self-reliance, originality, and kindliness, as our way of life encroaches on theirs.

What will become of the friends I left in North Greenland? I think about it a lot and I worry. They are among the most decent people on the face of the earth. The veneer of civilization has not reached them, and when it does I fear it will spoil them. I loved them all and I still do.

V

Diary, October 13 - December 31, 1913

I KEPT A DIARY for my personal use from October 13, 1913, until my birthday on June 1, 1914. I also kept field notes whenever I was in charge at headquarters or when I was on a major trip without MacMillan, leader of the expedition.

Etah, October 13, 1913

There are at Etah now about 40 Eskimos, or as they call themselves, Inuit. We have three families dependent on us, or rather we depend on them for meat and as dog drivers, and they on us for shelter, fuel, and some food, such as crackers, tea, salt, and whatever we have left from our meals. They have quarters in one corner of the storehouse, where we have made partitions of striped canvas. Each family has a room entirely lined with canvas; each room has a one-burner oil stove and a candle. The bedding consists entirely of skins: caribou, musk ox, bear, and seal. Some of the women have put up pictures that we have given them; before our time Eskimos had made no attempt at decoration.

All the other families live in stone huts, partly dug into the ground and partly built up with stones and turf. There are five of these igloos nearby: two on our right and three along the shore to the left, all so near that we could throw a stone past any one. There are one great grandfather, one grandfather, seven heads of families, and three nursing babies in the town, besides the usual number of boys and girls. All seem in good health and are very happy. Laughter is always near the surface. There seems to be no mental strain on even the wisest. The women are well treated and contented. On the whole, however, they do not seem to be in the same physical condition as the men, which would be natural since their mode of life keeps them indoors much of the time. Although the igloos are warm, they are not well ventilated, and the air is always close and damp.

Tonight perhaps a dozen natives called on us, as they are free to do at any time up to ten o'clock at night. We had games of all sorts: Up Jenkins, checkers, and cards, besides the Victrola. The quickness with which these people learn games is wonderful. Card tricks are easy for them, and they will watch a game of solitaire once or twice, then take the pack and play it off without any serious mistake.

Our arrival has not seemed to render the Eskimos less dependent on the game, which constitutes their sole food. One party returned last night from a three weeks' caribou hunt, during which time they shot 47. Part of this meat comes to us, and, judging by the steaks we had today, is very tender and good.

Until a few days ago, we have been working on our house, mostly inside for the last two weeks. The house proper is about square. Upon entering by the front door, one goes into a square central room with two windows facing the front. On either side there are two bedrooms. That on the right belongs to MacMillan alone. Next to that comes Tanquary's and Ekblaw's room. On the opposite side come first Small and Green, then Allen and me. Back of the main room there are the carpentry, electrical, and store rooms. In front and on the left side, there is a shed running the length of the house, all closed in.

There has been some hunting by various members of the party at odd times, mostly by me. We have bagged some 50 rabbits, the same number of ptarmigan, and 30 or 40 eider ducks. Ten walrus were shot before the *Erik* left. Now the bay is frozen over, and we hope to get a few seals as they come out on the ice to sleep. Tonight the thermometer has reached zero for the first time. Home seems a long way off.

The typewriter is set up this evening for the first time, and I am standing watch from ten until one. The watches are from ten to one, one to four, and four to seven, when the cook gets up. Breakfast is at nine, dinner at four; only two meals are served, but we can lunch if necessary.

Our wireless has been ready for about a week, but as yet no messages have been caught. We consider it very doubtful anyway that we shall get anything, as our outfit is not powerful. However, the electric lights are fine, and we will set up a telephone line to the nearby igloos.

The Eskimo women are gradually making fur clothing for us: boots of sealskin, and stockings, shirts, and coats of the sheepskin that we brought. The men are making sledges, *komatiks*, from material also brought by us. There is absolutely no dishonesty about these people, and they can be trusted with anything.

The sun leaves us in a few days and scarcely comes above the horizon now; it gives a sunset effect all day long. We have a remarkable assortment of books to read and study, and we look forward to any inactivity with anticipation rather than dread. The night watches are rather looked forward to also, as they afford time to read up on some subject, Arctic books taking preference.

Etah, October 18, 1913

Tanquary and Ahnowka went up to the glacier to visit their fox traps and will stay overnight in the snow igloo built there by Nookapingwa on his return home from the caribou hunt. They have Ahnowk's *komatik* with five dogs.

Panikpa and Kakotcheea on one *komatik*, and Meetak on another, left today for the caribou grounds, north, toward the Humboldt Glacier. They took with them as food a little tea and a frozen piece of walrus meat. Out of this, the dogs must be fed as well as the men, unless other game is secured, and they may be gone three weeks, as was the last party. Each man has a sleeping bag of musk-ox skin, a few extra skin clothes, and some robes. The thermometer last night was three below zero. The ice in the bay is solid now, and dog teams go at will anywhere upon it.

Ahpellah and Etookashoo have their *komatiks* finished. They are very good workmen and take considerable pride in their work. Ahtetah, Ahpellah's wife and an engaging girl, made a pair of sheepskin trousers for me this afternoon, with the wool on the outside. They are Eskimo style and come down only to just below the knee. I have given her one of Ruth's old hair ribbons. As a rule, the Arctic dressmaker prefers to sew in our rooms, but Ahtetah is an exception and seems to prefer her own quarters, possibly because of her two-year-old son. She is one of the best sewers, and energetic and careful as well.

Jot gave us some fine baked beans and Boston brown bread for dinner today. Green is at work taking observations to determine the exact time, which he thinks can be done within ten seconds of the correct time. No news as yet from the wireless, although Allen listens every night. He connected the igloos and the house by telephone today, to the great entertainment of the natives. They express no surprise now at whatever we do, although the electric lights drew a few exclamations at first. "*Now-i-o*" is their favorite term whenever anything worthy of note happens, and is given with a very friendly accent, as much as to say, "Will you look at that now." A more friendly and gentlemanly lot of people than these Polar Eskimos one cannot well expect to meet on this earth. Their absolute honesty seems remarkable to all of us.

They all smoke, and even the women smoke some. I have already given away two pipes in return for a whip and some moccasin laces.

We are rather lacking in the bearded or square flipper sealskins to make *kamik* soles from, and are looking forward to a trip to the next Eskimo settlement south in search of some. Here at Etah, seals are scarce and for the most part are only small ringed seals.

We had a session last night with Etookashoo and Ahpellah, the map of Sverdrup, and the book, *My Attainment of the Pole* (New York, 1911), of Dr. Frederick A. Cook, who claimed to have reached the North Pole before Peary. These two Eskimos were with Cook on his "North Pole" trip. Etookashoo agrees absolutely with Ahpellah as to the course they took and resolutely denies they were ever out of sight of land. Each of these two men traced the same course on the map, at different times, and without knowing the other had done so. They each declared separately that the party had four cartridges left when they arrived back in Greenland, whereas Cook declared they had none. They had no hardship whatever until nearly home.

The picture that Dr. Cook claimed was taken at the North Pole was located by them on the map, near Ellesmere Land, some 400 miles from the Pole. Walrus did not attack their canvas boat and thrust a tusk through it as Cook wrote in his book. The frank, open-faced manner with which these men answered our questions convinced us all of the truth of their story. We tried in vain to break down their testimony, but could not budge them.

Etah, October 19, 1913

Tanquary and Ahnowka came back from their overnight camping trip about dinnertime, or slightly after four o'clock. They reported a comfortable trip and fourteen hours' sleep in the snow igloo. Each shot one rabbit. I shot one near the house in the afternoon. The intestines of what game is brought in and cleaned at the house I get for my bitch and her puppies; also the scraps from the table, which are sometimes scanty. One of my pups is sick today and will have to be shot, I think. Both hind legs are useless, and he cries continually.

At noon Mac took our portraits with our sheepskin clothes on. The sun scarcely shows above the ice to the south and looks like a fire through the blowing snow.

Today being Sunday, as near as I can figure, we had for dinner a caribou roast with potatoes, cranberry sauce, and a gelatin pudding. This last was superfluous. One of the Eskimo boys played the Victrola during the meal, so we had a rather bang-up dinner.

Much to the amusement of the settlement, I harnessed up my one dog and started with the toboggan to get some supplies from Provision Point. She didn't want to leave her puppies, and as we each had traces attached to us, the toboggan was in danger of being torn apart. After I had dragged her half way, she decided to come my way, and the home trip found us both pulling together. The puppies will be big enough to be trained in a few months, but not until after the Crocker Land trip.

Several Eskimos, besides those we have engaged, have asked to go on the trip with us, and we will have no trouble in getting all the dog drivers we need.

Etah, October 20, 1913

Today has been occupied in sorting over the field supplies. The primus stove and the sledges are being overhauled with a view to several side trips after game and skins as soon as the ice will bear us along the shore to the south. One party of Eskimos plans a trip to the north after bear or foxes.

My sheepskin clothing is all made, but we still lack the proper skin to make *kamik* soles.

We weigh ourselves stripped every week from now on. I find I am the heaviest of the party and am heavier than at any time in years: 175 pounds at the first weighing. Strange to say I am not among the heaviest eaters. Also, I am trying to keep the blood pressure of each member. The compound microscope has not been satisfactory, and I have no great desire to do blood counting with it, especially as there is no mechanical stage. The hemoglobin estimation will be taken by the Tallquist method.

All the men are in fine trim physically and are eating well. Tanquary and Allen have each brought a 125-pound crate of flour from the point on a tump line, about a half-mile carry. All of us are snapping our whips in expectation of dog teams soon. The lashes are about 15 feet long and are of very light seal-hide strips. We find it difficult not to wind the lash about our necks.

Etah, October 21, 1913

Today has been cold and windy. I tried to get a rabbit. The wind and blowing snow made the work tough, and finally my mustache and beard became so iced up that I could not close my lips, so I came back to the house. The clothing is warm enough, but one's face certainly suffers when traveling upwind. We are not wearing any skin clothing yet. We must soon do so if the weather continues to grow colder.

Tonight the Eskimos were in watching us play cards, and later they played themselves amid much laughter. Today's dinner consisted of smothered rabbit hearts and livers, potatoes, and string beans, with peaches for dessert. Jot has a knack for making fine yeast bread. He has to make six loaves a day, and this morning he gave us a surprise in the shape of a Johnnie cake.

Etah, October 22, 1913

I have had to shoot my sick puppy; he could not walk. Tanquary has skinned him and is to examine the intestines for parasites. The seals, foxes, and gulls all have worms of different sorts.

It is my watch now, and Alnea is cooking a fox on the stove. She caught two today. We allow the Eskimos to cook when we are not using the stove. This saves oil, for our own Eskimos have been given kerosene stoves and use them for the double purposes of warmth and cooking.

Panikpa and Kakotcheea left for the caribou hunting grounds today, having returned from their first attempt because of high winds on the icecap. Ahnowka brought in one rabbit, the only one shot by three parties.

Ek is going to eat part of my puppy tomorrow at breakfast, or says he is. He cooked dinner today and gave us pea soup, with pears for dessert. For breakfast a big dish of buckwheat cakes with brown sugar disappeared.

It is six above tonight, but was eight below sometime tonight by the minimum thermometer. I am still wearing the low Britain moccasins I first put on the night of the wreck at Barge Point. They are the most serviceable footwear for this country except for very cold weather. I stuff the bottoms with dry grass before putting them on over two or three pairs of stockings.

Etah, October 27, 1913

We have had a warm day with no wind after the snowstorm of yesterday. All hands went hunting, getting three rabbits, and I shot one blue fox. The Eskimos sledged the whaleboat to the edge of the ice and launched it after walrus, but with no success.

Sipsoo has been knocking the back teeth out of some of his young dogs preparatory to tying them up for the first time. This is to prevent them from chewing the sealskin thongs with which they are fastened. It is not a nice thing to see or listen to, but it has to be done to have any teams at all.

Allen has charged the door latch of his room with electricity. It is a treat to watch the Eskimos try to open it.

Panikpa and Kakotcheea came home tonight with a load of *tuctu* or caribou skins and meat, but with no new game. We have enough caribou skins now to make each one a sleeping bag. The fresh skins are nailed to our ceiling and dried, three at a time. One of them is almost white, and all are much lighter in color than those from Labrador. Sipsoo is going north to Anoritok after bear as soon as weather permits. We need the skins for cold-weather pants.

I had a severe headache today, the first after a long time, and I went to bed as soon as I came in from hunting.

The thermometer has been up to 22 and down to 11 today. We were all uncomfortably warm in our windproof clothing.

My pictures of Ruth and Marion are growing more and more dear to me as time goes on. I have them carefully placed over my bunk so that I may see them on awakening. Oftentimes I wonder whatever I could have been thinking of when I left them for such a long time. I guess we are all thinking of home more than any of us tell.

Etah, October 29, 1913

The course of high tides has overflowed the ice enough to prevent the sledging of goods to any extent for a few days.

Sipsoo has bargained for an oil stove and has also paid one dog for a box of dog biscuits for his children.

All the women have fox traps set, about four miles from the house, far enough away not to catch the dogs. Both blue and white foxes are caught here. They are not as heavy as the rabbits we get, and yet the foxes prey on the rabbits. I have frosted the bridge of my nose underneath the metal of my glasses, and the skin is peeling. Mac has done the same to his cheeks.

Ahtetah finished my *kamiks* today, for which I gave her a dirty towel. That sounds bad, but it was not very dirty. Mac has given her two fine caribou skins with which to make me a *kooletah,* as the hooded jacket is called. These are too warm to work or travel in when walking, but are used when riding on the dog sledges and sometimes when sleeping. Mine is the first to be made, and my smiling seamstress has picked over all the skins and chosen the two best ones. She has made all my clothes so far and seems eager to do her best in as short a time as possible. All the women cut both cloth and skins with a knife like our chopping-tray knives. They are expert garment cutters, and that without any measuring tools. The hood is rimmed with a roll of fur or a fox tail to protect the face from the wind, and it usually has a drawstring. I am to have some bearskin pants made soon. These skins are what we lack most, and I am lucky to get them.

This morning I saw a small boy who had one leg partly useless. When I stripped him in a warm room I could see he had partial paralysis of the calf muscles. The ankle joint is wobbly, but he can move it in all directions. There are eight or ten small scars below the knee where, his mother tells me, he has had sores. She says the lameness has always been the same. I am going to see him again and if possible find out more about the case. I shall do all I can for him.

Also this morning I brought a 50-pound box of macaroni from Provision Point. Coming around by the shore, I fell several times on the rocks; in the half light one cannot see the depressions in the ground.

Ekblaw is cleaning the bathtub preparatory to taking his monthly bath. I have given up the tub and use a cloth and my wash basin. He has blistered two fingers scrubbing clothes tonight, and they are not very clean at that. Allen is just finding out that Ek has washed one of his, Allen's, pairs of stockings. I presume Ek will be some disgusted when he finds out the mistake.

Etah, November 2, 1913

The thermometer dropped to 14 below, and a bad north wind is blowing with clouds of drifting snow; nothing compared to what is to come, but it seems bad to us who have not seen any worse weather.

I gave Ahtetah and Alnea each a doll today for work done for me, and gave Ahtetah a knife for a pair of rabbit skin stockings. The doll with moveable eyes paid for the whole *kooletah.* Also I have a pair of mittens made from the skin of the puppy I shot. My bearskin pants came back from the tailor, and in payment I gave Alningwa my old mud raincoat and a ring. The trading material Marion gave me is very handy. Although Mac pays for us all in material provided by the Museum, I think I get the worth of things given and am surely getting more clothes made and in shorter order than the rest. At any rate I feel better if I give them something myself.

The caribou *kooletah* is very well made. The back and hood are all one piece, the hood being the head of the animal, with the ears on and standing out in a lifelike manner. Around the face, and fitted with draw strings, is a roll of the same skin, which protects me from the wind remarkably. Over each shoulder is a darker piece, and the breast is almost pure white. All the skin is in prime condition with thick, long hair.

Before sewing, the women chew all these skins, softening them and making them more pliable.

I put on my skin clothing and went out to test the suit for warmth. I think I can see that we will not suffer as severely from the cold as I first feared. The clothes are astonishingly warm. The pants especially are of very heavy fur and a rather thick skin, which makes them stiff to walk in as well as warm. We are all now using grass in our *kamiks* as the Eskimos do. The weight of the clothes to be worn in the coldest weather is sixteen pounds.

Tonight the Eskimos gave us a concert. Two sing at a time, one beating time with a stick on a tin plate, and all the while swinging the body from side to side.

Etah, November 5, 1913

Mac and Allen went up to Littleton Island with two *komatiks* this morning and found many caches of eider duck eggs. It seems as if these Eskimos live with a stock of eggs the year round. We have tried them and find them excellent. They were gathered in June and are now frozen hard as rocks. There are thousands stored under rocks on the island, and some ducks also.

The ice is reported to be solid to the south, and we expect visitors from the Eskimo settlements there.

This evening I have made some jack-wax from the maple syrup Father gave me. You boil the syrup down until it makes small balls if dropped in cold water, then pour it on the snow. This hardens into excellent taffy. The men found it much to their taste. We have about a hundred pounds of maple sugar in our stores.

Ek and Tank are at their evening game of chess, hammer and tongs. They are about even, but both are very careless. Mac, Jot, and Green play too, but no one has played as much as I or is my equal. Meetak, Etookashoo, Ahpellah, Peeawato, and Tungwe are playing fan-tan on the dining table with poker chips. Jot has hung a bunch of unplucked ptarmigan over the stove to thaw out for tomorrow's dinner. Ahtetah has nailed a fresh caribou skin to the ceiling, and Alnea is thawing one at the back of the stove. On the rack over the stove are numerous garments drying. I can see stockings, both sheepskin and woolen, mittens, *kamiks,* and *kooletahs.* A small sealskin is tacked to the ceiling over my head. Jot is knitting a salmon net in one corner of the room; according to a report, there is a run of salmon here in the spring.

Etah, November 10, 1913

Furious winds and cold. Today I wore the sheepskin *kooletah* with a big face roll of caribou hair and was the only one who didn't freeze his cheeks. We brought the last of the food over from Provision Point. All the Eskimos worked with us and were fed at our table afterward. There is a steep bank in front of the house. It is no light job to get a 100-pound crate up it, and some of the crates are heavier. Mac found the missing ink box with everything in good order, although frozen solid. The coffee grinder came to light in the same box.

I finished my *komatik* today in a blaze of glory, with Eskimos scrubbing at the rust on the steel shoes. The parts went together nicely, but the bolts coming up through the runners to the top rail were bothersome to head up, as there were no nuts.

The attic and everything in it is covered with thick, white frost. Water in my room is dripping from the ceiling onto my blankets, so I have them out before the stove to dry and am getting my rubber blanket to cover the bed afterward. I have sewed my five blankets together and find them none too warm.

I found a louse on me for the first time. I expect it came from the Eskimo child I had on my bed to examine his lame leg. None of the other men has looked yet to see if he is lousy, but I suspect they all are.

Today is Mac's birthday. We had a cake with colored candles and after dinner put the spigot in the whisky cask for the first time. Fitz and I had written some verses. It was a merry evening.

Etah, November 17, 1913

Tomorrow I am going south about twenty miles, to Sulwuddy, walrus hunting with Etookashoo and Ahpellah. We may stay five days. There is a moon now.

List of things to take tomorrow:

blue flame oil stove, with pot and snow melter, 1 cup, 1 spoon, 1 can opener, 1 funnel,
2 boxes matches, 2 gallons oil, 6 candles, 1 tent with fly and pole,
1 sheepskin *kooletah* to wear generally,
1 caribou skin *kooletah* to sleep in or wear on the sledge,
1 pr. *kamiks*, 1 pr. Britain moccasins,
1 pr. bearskin pants,
2 pr. sheepskin stockings, 1 pr. rabbit skin,
2 pr. woolen; 1 rifle (.33 caliber Winchester),
2 boxes cartridges, 1 pr. field glasses, 1 thermometer,
1 compass, 1 notebook and pencil,
1 sleeping bag, 1 hunting knife.

Provisions:

3 cans beans	2 bags tea
3 cans hash	1 bag sugar
6 cans deviled sausage	3 cans milk
4 cans clam chowder	25 lb. white crackers [hardtack or ship biscuit]
6 packages tobacco for Ahpellah and Etookashoo	

Sulwuddy, November 18, 1913

Etookashoo, Ahpellah, and I had breakfast together at six. Half an hour later we were under way across the harbor headed south. At Cape Alexander we went overland a short distance across a glacier, then onto the ice on foot again.

The ice foot is a thick ledge of ice and snow that forms between the land and the sea ice. It is the road used by the Eskimos and their dogsleds whenever possible. It is usually safe, flat, smooth, and good going. Wind and currents often pile the sea ice into pressure ridges or split it with leads of open water.

Here for some distance the sea ice had not formed strongly enough to bear us, and we kept to the ice foot for perhaps two miles. Upon entering the mouth of a bay, the ice seemed better, and we crossed it on the sea ice with no trouble.

We caught up with three other Eskimos with as many dog teams, going to the same place we were. They had a rock and sod igloo there at Sulwuddy that they banked up with snow and moved into upon arriving. I cooked our first meal while my party was building a snow house, which they seemed to prefer to my tent. My stove worked well, and before the Eskimos were through with the snow igloo we had tea and beans. It took about an hour to get our quarters habitable, but I found it time well spent. The Eskimo soapstone blubber lamp kept us warm and lighted the interior so well that I did not need the candles I had brought to read by. After changing my foot gear, I went to bed with all my skin clothes on inside my blanket sleeping bag. The other two had musk ox bags and took off all their clothes. I was cold at first but later warmed up and slept well.

Sulwuddy, November 19, 1913

After breakfast at six we went four miles out on the ice with dog teams, looking for walrus. We heard some bellowing farther out but could not get to them. On the way back, I took Ahpellah's team to the igloo while he waited at a seal hole, coming in later with a square-flipper or bearded seal, an *ooksuk*.

Sulwuddy, November 20, 1913

The temperature outside our igloo was 10 below zero, while inside it was 30 above. There was apt to be a little drip when my cooking stove was in use, and over the stove the wall thinned out somewhat. After breakfast my companions went out to some seal holes and were away all day. Ahpellah again succeeded in getting a big *ooksuk;* Etookashoo got nothing.

I had been out on the ice by myself all day and saw many fresh holes where seals had come up to breathe. On coming back I tried my hand at lighting the stone lamp, with success, although it smoked some. The moss wick must first be thoroughly rubbed up and almost powdered, then carefully spread along the edge of the lamp so as to touch the oil as it is melted from the blubber. A small piece of the fat is first melted and dripped over the wick. This is then lighted, and by its own heat it in turn melts enough oil from the blubber to keep burning indefinitely, as long as there is some blubber in the lamp.

Etah, November 21, 1913

In the morning we started back to headquarters with a load of sealskins and arrived about two o'clock.

Etah, December 1, 1913

Dark all the time.

We have a few visitors who came on the full moon, from the settlements south of us. Today Mene Wallace came to the house. He is the Eskimo who was educated in New York some years ago, and who afterward had to leave the United States against his will. He seems to be in good health and prosperous. He is to stay with us. He talks both Eskimo and English well and will be a help to us in learning the language. He reports a sick child at Umanak, 150 miles south, and Mac has given me leave to go see it. The new moon comes this Friday, and possibly Mene and I will go then.

We are playing chess quite a lot, sleeping a lot, and having rather a good time with so much company. I have offered a pair of good woolen stockings to the first man to win one chess game in 20 from me, and am having my hands full. I am playing with the greatest circumspection, needless to say.

Monday, Allen and I cleaned all the goods out of our room and put the big oil stove in to melt the ice and frost from the walls and ceiling. The water dripped furiously for a while. Our room is the wettest of all and the coldest, as shown by the thermometer. We have stuffed the cracks as well as possible and covered the windows with double thicknesses of heavy paper.

Jot has a large piece of caribou meat on the shelf thawing, and we have made quite a hole in it, eating it raw.

Etah, December 4, 1913

Today and tomorrow will be getting-ready days for the trip to Umanak: food, oil, stoves, clothes, matches, sleeping bags, etc. I shall probably be staying with Eskimos all the time and may get meat from them.

Nerky, December 6, 1913

At eight Mene, Ootah, and I were off for Umanak, or Thule, as Freuchen and Rasmussen have named it, with Nerky as the first stopping place. We traveled over the sea ice down the coast, going over the glacier behind Cape Alexander to avoid open water. We arrived at Nerky at five p.m. I went into Inyougeeto's igloo, which is large and well kept, and as they have no children, especially good to sleep in. The igloo was very well lighted by three stone lamps, and we were as warm as one cares to be. I heated some canned food, made tea, and later the Eskimos cooked a big pot of seal meat for me.

Keato, December 7, 1913

Left Nerky at nine a.m. and traveled ten hours across the bay to the island of Keato, where there are four igloos. The dogs were somewhat footsore, but trotted at perhaps five miles an hour the whole time. I put up at Pooadloona's igloo, and as he had recently shot two bears, asked for some bear meat to be cooked. It is considered a great treat here. He brought in the foreleg and shoulder of an immense animal, and after letting it thaw some, cut steaks from the best parts and stewed them. Everybody had all they could eat. I find no discomfort in eating Eskimo fashion: taking the meat in the fingers, fastening the teeth into it, and cutting it off with a knife as near the lips as one dares.

En route, Keato to Umanak, December 8, 1913

At Keato I found a man with both legs partially useless. He had been totally paralyzed two years ago while on a hunting trip, the trouble coming on in a day's time. He has some movement in the legs now, but little strength. The sphincters are not affected. I told him to come to Etah, and I would do what I could for him when I got back. Saw Nellica and Metik.

Akkommodingwa is traveling with us from Nerky to Umanak to carry some meat to his uncle, who has been sick two months.

We left Keato at noon and traveled until one a.m., sleeping in a snow house the rest of the night. During the trip we saw many bear tracks, but as the dogs did not care to follow them, they must have been old.

Umanak, December 9, 1913

Had a comfortable night. Left at eleven a.m. and got to Umanak at nine p.m. The dogs' feet were bleeding some, but they went at the same pace all day.

Here I found Ooblooya in bed after two months with rheumatism. His left knee and elbow are swollen and painful; otherwise he is the picture of health. I also saw a girl of about twelve who seemed to have had typhoid fever. She had been sick about a month, some of the time out of her head, and had become very thin. There have been a number of similar cases recently among the children, but none have died.

I slept well in Ooblooya's igloo in spite of his three young children.

Umanak, December 10, 1913

Had breakfast of tea and dog biscuit at seven a.m. Moved to the house of the missionaries, who are South Greenland Eskimos and have gone to Upernavik for the winter. I found two good stoves and plenty of coal. I built a fire in each and keep them going all the time. I am expecting a man to come with two fingers to be amputated, but the wind blows so hard that he cannot travel today.

Umanak, December 11, 1913

The man came, and with Mene's assistance with the ether, and by the light of the dim Eskimo lamps, I took off one finger from each hand. These had been shattered some months before by an exploding rifle cartridge and were stiff, useless, and in the way. He took ether well.

Umanak, December 12, 1913

Rasmussen is expected back from the south anytime now, and, as the dogs' feet need time to heal, I am staying a day or two longer. Mene obtained four loons today. They tasted rather strong, but I had no trouble in eating my share. Egingwa gave me a large trout, about four pounds, which I boiled. He also cooked a white fox, which was pretty bad. I was glad I had the trout.

En route Umanak to Kangerdlookswa, December 15, 1913

Rasmussen had not come, but we had been gone long enough. Left at eight in the morning with Mene, Egingwa, and Koodlookto; traveled about ten hours; slept in a snow igloo with them.

Kangerdlookswa, December 16, 1913

Started at three a.m. over the glacier to Whale Sound, and after going ten miles came down onto sea ice again. There Koodlookto left us on his way north toward Igloodahourny, while Egingwa, Mene, and I went off to the east toward Kangerdlookswa, where we arrived at five p.m. I put up in Ootah's igloo. This is about three times as large as any other I have seen. The roof is of lumber covered with sod and grass. The ridge pole was obtained from Dr. Cook. I had a fine supper of seal meat and narwhal skin, or *mattak*. It had been a long day, fourteen hours with no food or rest, and food was welcome. We will give tomorrow to the dogs to get rested.

Egingwa and Ootah, brothers, two of Peary's North Pole Eskimos and fine men, are the most prosperous Eskimos I have come across. They have dishes, tools, and wood in abundance. Egingwa's wife washes her face and combs her hair every morning.

Etah, December 19, 1913

Yesterday we left Kangerdlookswa at five a.m. for Igloodahourny; arrived at seven p.m. The going was good, and we traveled right along all day.

There I learned Allen was sick at Etah, and Mac had sent word I was needed for him. After one hour's sleep I started with Nookapingwa and a light sledge for Etah. At Nerky we stopped two hours and then continued on through the night.

Arrived at Etah at nine this morning, having traveled steadily 25 out of the last 28 hours. The dogs did well. Home again. The food tastes good. Everything looks good. Allen is better. He had an acute attack of kidney congestion with a fever of 104, bloody urine, and much pain in the back. I find now some blood corpuscles, a small amount of albumen, and numerous casts in the urine. Spg 1.020. Temp. 100. I am limiting his diet and keeping him in bed until the urine clears up some.

Etah, December 21, 1913

The man with the paralyzed legs whom I saw at Keato is here. I am looking him over and have fitted a pair of crutches for him.

Eight sledge loads of visitors left for their homes today. They had crowded us some, and, as we gave them tea and crackers twice daily, it kept us pretty busy.

Jot and Tank are away, and Ek does the cooking very well. I look after the hot water, wash the dishes, and keep things clean generally. Jot had left things in a mess and very dirty.

Mac reports the advance supplies sent north to Anoritok were cached quickly, and another trip taken with light loads across Smith Sound to Cape Sabine on Pim Island, Ellesmere Land, a thing we had hardly hoped could be done this early. All this is in preparation for our Crocker Land trip. On this excursion four bears were shot, which will keep us supplied with skins and meat for some time.

Etah, December 25, 1913, Christmas Day

We popped some corn, and the Eskimo girls threaded it so it could be used for decorations. Some fake evergreens and ribbons completed the attempt to make the room seem like home on this day. The dinner, which President Osborn of the Museum had put up for the occasion, came through in good shape, except the wine, which was frozen, the bottle broken. Jot and Tank arrived from the south just as dinner was being served, so we were all together.

Later in the evening the presents were given out. All the Eskimos were there, about 54, making 61 in all. The presents of candy and chewing gum for the Eskimos were in a large bag, which they each in turn reached into and took one package from. Afterwards they were given packages of tobacco and cigarettes. Last of all, a large fruitcake was cut into 61 pieces.

Etah, December 27, 1913

Each day gets noticeably lighter now.

Esayu came in with two other sledges today. He has had for some years past a stricture of the urethra and has come to be helped if possible. His wife got gonorrhea from the crew of a whaling ship about four years ago. In the evening, I gave him ether and succeeded in passing a sound up to 28 F. in size. The bladder was full when he arrived and possibly would have ruptured in a few days. He is doing well and will stay for treatment. Esayu is one the the most gentlemanly and trustworthy men I have ever met, an elderly man, extremely thoughtful in camp and resourceful in the field. He was of great value to Peary and is also to us.

Esayu is the third Polar Inuit I have treated for the same symptoms with the same cause: venereal disease, which has now burned itself out, brought to them by our Christian civilization. The other two are already the proud possessors and demonstrators of an unusually free flow of urine. I hope the treatment will be lasting. Otherwise we all know their fate without surgical help: a painful death from uremia or a ruptured bladder.

The whole tribe, from Cape York to Etah, needs medical attention badly. While I am here I shall be their *nagorsak*, or doctor, as they have none. This is not in my contract, so the requirements of the expedition must always come first, but when I can, I shall go wherever I am called. A physician should be sent here whenever conditions make it possible. A small lying-in hospital is needed, as the death rate of both mothers and newborns is extremely high.

Etah, December 31, 1913

Another dark day and no traveling.

In the evening firecrackers and a midnight feed of cake.

VI

Diary, January 1 - June 1, 1914

Etah, January 1, 1914

A new year. It seems possible we will not all be here next New Year's Day. I would a thousand times rather be home today!

Early in February we shall leave for Crocker Land, going first north to Anoritok, then crossing Smith Sound, Ellesmere Land, and the Polar Sea. The trip will be a hard one, with unforeseen dangers. To tell the truth, I rather dread the start. The cold, the danger, and the privations are not pleasant to look forward to, yet I know that once we are under way, the bustle and hurry of the trail will take up all our attention.

We may venture too far on Crocker Land to get back the same season, and ice in Smith Sound may possibly break up early enough to prevent our crossing over from Ellesmere Land on our return. Fuel and food will be cached near Cape Sabine in case of such an emergency. I have suggested that enough food be put there by the remaining Eskimos while we are gone to Crocker Land to enable a party to stay in Ellesmere Land all summer. Game is abundant there, and the ice does not cover the land as in Greenland.

Here there are no cliques as yet. The men are good companions, when we give in some to each other's idiosyncrasies. Allen and I have had no squabbles yet, which cannot be said of the other roommates. Mac sleeps mostly out in a snow igloo, and there is an Eskimo family often in his room. Sometimes I sleep out, too. The house is constantly full of visitors. The air could not be worse. I have urged better ventilation, but with no results. Mac does not take advice in a good spirit.

Etah, January 3, 1914

The moon has begun to show again, and by the time it is gone we will be able to travel by the light of the sun in the middle of the day, although it will not be above the horizon. The full winter moon remains above the horizon more than half the time. In clear weather, visibility is excellent, shadows sharp. Gleaming snow adds its own light to that of the moon and stars. Precipitation is scant, but blowing snow and a thick, low fog are common. An Arctic whiteout envelops one in nothingness.

Today is clear and sparkling. Ekblaw and Koodlookto have gone south with several other Eskimos who had been waiting for new ice to form after it had been broken up by the recent storms. Koodlookto will show Ek a meteorite he has found, and they hope to bring back a piece of it.

We are all writing letters. The mail goes on its way soon by Eskimo dog team to Upernavik. Thence it is taken to Denmark next summer sometime, and from there to the States. Before he left, Ek wrote a letter to my little girl!

Letter from Ekblaw to Ruth Hunt:

ETAH, NORTH GREENLAND
January, 1914

My dear Miss Ruth:

Because I like your papa more and more, and because I am sure he is too modest to tell you how much good he is doing among these pleasant people of the Northland who have not usually any good doctor to take care of them, I am writing this letter from our house at Etah where we are now getting ready for the dash to Crocker Land, which begins soon — February seventh. I hope both you and your mamma will be glad to know that we are all just as well as can be, thanks to your papa's sensible care of us, and that we couldn't possibly be physically better ready to start out on the long, hard trip.

Your papa is a good angel to the sick people of the tribe. They all love him, and from Cape Melville to Etah — the entire range of the Smith Sound Eskimo — a route over which I have already traveled by moonlight with a dog sled — they have all heard of him, ask about him, and want to see him. You can easily imagine how much they need a doctor sometimes. When you write to your papa tell him that a great old Burgomaster gull from Brother John's Glacier near Etah came along one day and told you all about how your papa is cutting off decayed toes and fingers, curing sick eyes, sick throats, and all kinds of sick bodies.

I've killed two big polar bears, great, big old bears. And I've had trousers and boots and mittens made of their thick, white skins. Isn't that funny — to kill my own trousers! I've slept in a lot of igloos, and one night when a great storm caught us out on the ice and almost carried us out to the wild Atlantic, we slept in a small hole in a high cliff. There was a small, one-year-old girl in our party, and I was afraid she would freeze to death, but when morning came she was gurgling and cooing as happily as ever.

I think your papa has been very lonesome for his little girl, though he doesn't say much about it. He has your picture stuck up on the door of his room where he can see it all the time. I think I look at it almost as often as he. I would give almost the whole world for a little girl like you.

Loyally yours,
W. Elmer Ekblaw

Etah, January 16, 1914

Have been sick and in bed with the flu: high fever, severe headache, cough, vomiting freely. All well again now. Eskimos who have been in South Greenland brought the contagion with them.

Etah, January 26, 1914

Yesterday, Tank and I, with five Eskimos, took loads of pemmican and milk to the cache at Anoritok in the teeth of a cold north wind. We slept in snow igloos, uncomfortably, as we took no heating stoves and the weather was snapping cold. Wind and driving snow made hunting impossible, so we came home today.

Etah, January 29, 1914

South Greenland Eskimos have brought mumps and more coughs and colds to Etah. All the Eskimos are miserable. They cough and spit incessantly, and are not careful where they spit. Ek has mumps, and I expect it to spread to nearly all the Eskimos. That may well make trouble for the long trip.

The idea now is for the white men to walk, with no teams. The Eskimo sleds are to carry all the provisions. MacMillan is the only one of us to have a dog team. I do not approve of this but cannot change it. MacMillan is trading for foxskins to take home for himself, giving in exchange tea, sugar, biscuit, tobacco, matches, and other articles. I should prefer to have him purchase dogs and traveling outfits for the men. He does not ask advice or take any when offered by any of us.

It seems likely that, barring accidents, Mac, Ek, and Green will be the ones to go through to Crocker Land. Tanquary and I may get to the records south of Cape Thomas Hubbard and at Cape Colgate. I think frostbite may alter the program, however. In that case I would have to come back with the invalid. Even with three pairs of *kamiks*, one cannot keep stockings dry if one has to follow a dog team continuously, day after day. The pace is too fast.

All are ambitious to do some good traveling and are eager for the trip to begin.

Today, I examined a woman and tentatively diagnosed cancer of the uterus. It is tragic that I can do nothing for her. She will die this winter, I think. I shall try to get the specimen.

[The following is from a talk Hal gave some years later to a Medical Society meeting:]

> I did get that specimen but had a hell of a time getting it, and it didn't do me any good. She died at her home in Umanak that summer, and when sledging became good the next winter I went down, asked permission from her husband to open the grave, and did so. It was an extremely undesirable job. Putrefaction had set in, although now the body was frozen. There was no sunlight, and a bitter wind was pouring down the steep hillside where the grave was. I made a frozen section through the pelvis with a common carpenter's rip saw, went into that rotting body with my bare hands, and brought a slab back to headquarters, only to have the dogs break into the storehouse and gobble it up. It was the only cancer I saw all

the time I was in Greenland. I was sorely disappointed to be unable to confirm my clinical impression in the laboratory.

Etah, February 6, 1914

An explosion of gasoline burned Tauchingwa's face last night; not severely, however. He had mistaken it for kerosene and filled an oil stove with it.

Etah, February 7, 1914

Green and three Eskimos left today for the main trip, the other parties to follow daily as seems expedient. The first day's march is to be to the snow houses at Anoritok. Then we will go across Smith Sound and Ellesmere Land, and Mac's division will cross the Polar Sea to the great cliffs Peary saw in the distance. I shall travel with Ooblooya, who has slight rheumatism, and Tauchingwa, whose face will need to be protected.

Payer Harbor, Pim Island, Ellesmere Land, February 11, 1914

Tanquary left the eighth, Ekblaw the ninth, and I yesterday, facing a heavy wind with driving snow all the way to Anoritok. Today we crossed Smith Sound to Peary's old hut at Payer Harbor on Pim Island, near the Greely Starvation Camp at Cape Sabine. The ice was smooth, with two inches of snow on it. To our surprise, we found Ekblaw's division in the hut, as he had been snowbound for a day at Anoritok. Ek had Peary's old stove red-hot and soon gave us tea and pemmican stew.

Cache B, Cape Rutherford, Ellesmere Land, February 12, 1914

Both divisions left together today, two sleeps behind the foremost. Ek and I started out in advance of the sledges so as not to have to run to keep up, but they caught us after a few miles. The dogs, if not loaded too heavily, travel at a pace slightly faster than one can walk with heavy clothing and uneven footing. One perspires freely and occasionally is forced to ride for short distances on account of short breath or fatigue. On such occasions, the dogs slow down and the team falls behind rapidly. Up through Rice Strait we faced a severe north wind, but later it became calm.

At Cache B, where the advance party slept, we found no snow houses, so we slept that night behind a shelter of boxes. MacMillan has a full-length bag, and I have one of three-quarters length, but the others are supplied with half-length bags, the caribou *kooletah* supposedly sufficient for the upper part of the body. This is not a good rig and cannot be slept in comfortably. Each man has a small piece of fur to put under the bag. MacMillan has a musk-ox skin. The Eskimos have their own outfits, which are, in all cases except that of MacMillan, better than ours.

Ek and I worried and shivered through the night after a fashion. I could feel him shivering whenever I awoke, as we lay back to back. We were glad to get up in the morning.

[There must have been northern lights that night. One night many years later we were camping at Chimney Pond, in the crook of Mt. Katahdin. Hal woke us up at midnight to see the whole sky blazing with northern lights, shooting up from the ragged edges of the spruce trees to the north and from the mountains to our south. He threw a log on the fire and talked about that night in the Arctic. The Knife Edge became the forbidding cliffs of the far north, and the dying fire, the cold comfort of an Eskimo seal oil lamp.]

That's one trip we'll never forget, Ek and I. It must have been 50 below, maybe more. Ek wore his *kooletah* while traveling. Once in a while he'd push his hood back, and I would see the sweat on his bald head and told him: "You had better take off your *kooletah* and put on your blanket shirt and windproof." That's what I was wearing. If active, you're warm enough. When you are quiet you take them off and put on your *kooletah*. Ekblaw was heavy-built and short-legged. He was sturdy all right, but he worked when he walked. There was a vicious wind, and Ek did not want to change, so he wore his *kooletah* all day, ten hours.

At night there was no good snow to make a snow house, and we did not have good sleeping bags. The best we could do was to put up a windbreak of boxes and pemmican. Ek's *kooletah* was wet with sweat, and when he took it off all he had was the blanket shirt and the windproof. He lay on his *kooletah* all night. I don't remember what else he had, but we lay back to back, and I could feel Ek shivering. Just as long as he shivered I knew he was alive. In the morning his jacket was frozen solid, flat. He tried to put it on over his head and get his arms into the armholes, but it took him so long to get his hands into the stiff sleeves that he froze his fingers. As soon as he got into it he was all right. Exercise warmed him up, even his fingers, but he told me: "I'll never do that again, Hal."

Ek and I got along well together. We liked each other, and in the summer we had many a tramp together up on the hills back of the house. He was a geologist, botanist, and ornithologist. Later on, when I was the first to find the nest and eggs of the knot, until then never seen, I could see he was downcast. He would have liked to have been the first to find it, but he never showed it afterwards. He did not know envy or jealousy.

Beyond Alexandra Fiord, Ellesmere Land, February 13, 1914

In the tracks of the preceding party, we took to the ice foot and followed its windings all day long. The last high tides had overflowed the ice here, and it helped a lot to get off the soft snow of the day before. We passed the sleeping place of the leading party some distance before turning in for the night. Tonight we are again sleeping in the open. The worst of this is that one has no chance to dry one's foot gear, which becomes moist from sweat during the day.

Same, February 14 and 15, 1914

In the morning I found Etookashoo had the mumps. His testicles were affected, making it impossible for him to continue. I volunteered to stay with him while the others went on. After seeing the others off, I went back in the hills to look for game but found none.

The days are still very short. The sun has not come above the horizon, and to the south one sees a sunset effect all day. These are lonesome days, with nothing to do and lots of spare time to think of home folks. In the morning I arise as soon as color comes in the east, heat water for tea, and at the same time warm the frozen pemmican a little. Then I sing out to the invalid and ask if he wants food. This is needless, but the way he says yes always makes me smile, so I always do it. He lies on a sled in his musk-ox bag, bare naked, and I have not seen him up for two days, but guess he does get out sometimes. I take him a pint of red-hot tea, eight crackers, and his lump of pemmican. When I ask if he wants more, he always says yes, in a loud voice, so I have increased his allowance. I think he is getting well. After our meal I chop up a can of dog pemmican and distribute it. This I do twice daily, and the remainder of the day I try to keep warm and cheerful.

South Coast of Hayes Fiord, February 16, 1914

Etookashoo said he guessed he could travel some, so we started out. I left a pair of snowshoes and a 50-pound box of biscuits, as Etookashoo has to ride. He showed good pluck and was very cheerful as far as I could judge. We made slow progress all day, but finally made the same march as Ek. The dogs and I were about all in. No shelter here either, and I shall now snuggle up to the base of a steep cliff and bed down on the ice by myself. The stove gives some trouble here because of the wind.

Hayes Fiord, mouth of Bitestead Fiord, February 17, 1914

We got under way rather late, and about noon MacMillan, Mene, and Peeawahto caught up with us, as Etookashoo is still riding. Shortly we came upon the advance parties encamped in three snow houses on the ice in Hayes Fiord.

Several of the Eskimos are sick. The dogs are not in good condition, and the dog pemmican gives them diarrhea. The Eskimos want to go back, possibly to start over again. MacMillan has decided to do this, leaving Green and me to follow with Sipsoo and Ahpellingwa, who now have mumps and orchitis.

Same, February 18, 1914

In the early morning, Green and I were left here with the sick men. The others, traveling with light sledges, and thus able to ride, will reach Payer Harbor tonight. All provisions are left here, ready to be picked up on the next try for Crocker Land.

Payer Harbor, February 19, 1914

The Eskimos being sufficiently recovered, we also left, Fitz and I acting as ambulance drivers. We made Peary's hut in one march, although long after dark. I have blisters on both feet, as I walked all the way, probably about 40 miles. [The distance is 50 miles on Operational Navigation Chart ONC B-8.] It takes all there is in a man to keep up with one of these Eskimo dog teams, and I have done it enough to dislike it very much. The bear-skin pants do not allow the free swing of the legs necessary for rapid walking, and one perspires freely and uncomfortably in them.

Payer Harbor, February 20 and 21, 1914

We found the supply of coal, left by Peary, all used up, but managed to break up enough wood to get a fire started. The dogs were tired out, so although the day was fine with no wind, we stayed in camp. During the next night, a heavy wind sprang up and by morning traveling was out of the question. These Arctic winds are sudden and fierce. The snow drifts freely, and one is helpless, as in a thick fog.

[Afterwards, in his warm home, Hal remembered that cold and lonely time he had written about in his diary, February 14-20, and told us about it.]

> Oh, I was a homesick and unhappy man waiting for Etookashoo to get well. I didn't see him come out of his bag for three whole days, but I guess he must have, for I was feeding him heartily each day. He would stick an arm out to get his food and disappear with it immediately. I had nothing to do. The snow was too soft to make a snow house. When I had fed him, I tucked him into his warm musk-ox bag and tried to hunt. There was only a little light for a short time each day, and although I could see rabbit tracks, I could not see the rabbits. We had plenty of tea, crackers, and pemmican for the dogs and for us, but meat would have been good. To sleep I put my snowshoes down and a small piece of bear skin on them, and I lay down in my half-length bag behind a boulder to keep the wind off my face. I have had warmer bedfellows than that rock, but none I shall ever remember better. It was very cold. It seemed to me the nights were unnecessarily long.
>
> When Etookashoo said he would try to travel, I lashed him on the sledge, gave him the whip, pushed the sled, and off we started. The dogs did not know me, and they were ugly.
>
> At Hayes Fiord we met Mac and his party, with more sick men. They could not go on, so Mac went home to prepare for a second try. Green and I stayed with the sick men, and when they could travel we made Peary's hut on Pim Island in one day. Mac said to me later: "You went on foot from Hayes Fiord to Pim Island in one march! It is 50 miles!" I do not think it is that far. The dogs were heading home. My sick man was riding, but I kept trotting and walking all day. I could feel two hot places on my feet and I knew I was getting blisters. I stopped and changed my footgear, but when I got in there were two whopping big blisters. I put adhesive on them and had no more trouble. I can't believe I walked as far as Bangor to Hancock [40 miles] in one day.
>
> The hut was cold, and we needed wood to start a fire. There were some wooden coffins outside, with dead Eskimos inside, dead for many years. No one objected when I pried one open, and finding only a skeleton, chopped up the wood of the coffin for kindling.

Anoritok, Greenland, February 22, 1914

Although the wind had abated somewhat, the air was still filled with clouds of drifting snow. The Eskimos were willing to go, however, and in the forenoon we started across Smith Sound, making land at Anoritok about dark. The trip had not been as windy as expected, except near land on both sides. We found the snow houses intact and piled into the biggest. My feet were still sore and blistered.

Etah, February 23, 1914

I started out ahead of the teams and got nearly to Littleton Island before they overtook me. At Sunrise Point, Fitz and I went overland while the teams followed the ice foot. We came into headquarters ahead of the Eskimos, since the distance was shorter.

Etah, February 24, 1914

Allen has mumps. Tanquary and I have sore feet. I think Tank frosted one of his toes, but possibly it came from the chafing of a snowshoe thong. I also have a cough and sore throat. During the trip, several of the Eskimos were coughing incessantly. The room is full of drying clothes. I shall not get a chance to put mine up for a week.

Etah, February 25, 1914

Fitz, Ek and I are taking 12-hour watches, with Allen sick and Tank unable to get out to the thermometer shelter because of his sore foot. The readings are taken every hour for temperature. I can see no reason for this, but Mac says they will be "interesting." My feet are not bad, but there are several blisters the size of a silver dollar. I am taking good care of them and am putting dressings on Tank's toe, as it is infected.

Etah, March 1-5, 1914

MacMillan, Green, and Ekblaw are getting ready for the second attempt. Each is to have his own team this time. The Eskimos are at Peteravik hunting walrus for dog food instead of pemmican.

There is a white wolf here that followed the teams from Ellesmere Land, the first seen around Etah for some time.

Etah, March 11, 1914

MacMillan, Green, Ekblaw, Peeawahto, Mene, and Etookashoo left today for Crocker Land. Four other Eskimos left yesterday. MacMillan has left me in charge at headquarters. We are feeding the families of the men who have gone on the trip, which makes it unpleasant in the house, because they have free run of the main room and are noisy. Our bedrooms are not warm enough to sit in during the winter, and are so damp that we need to keep kerosene stoves burning under the bunks.

Etah, March 15, 1914

As usual, very windy. After breakfast the Eskimos reported that the wolf was nearby. Jot and I shot at it from the front of the house. Jot's second shot apparently broke a leg; the wolf sat down and bit at the wound, afterwards making off on three legs. I shot once, missing. Jot again hit, but the wolf made off. We are not bad shots, but we were not close; we wanted to get that wolf before he did any harm.

We then went in to get warmer clothing, and after following a short distance, I found the wolf lying down, badly hurt. It ran, however, and I was forced to shoot it from behind. It lay down, but the poor beast was only crippled in the hind legs, and the intestines were dragging. I shot once into the side of the head, killing the wolf instantly. We dragged it to the house on a sledge, took pictures, and weighed and measured it. As we had thought some days ago, it was a female. It weighed 57 pounds, the fur was in fine condition and all white, though somewhat dirty. Total length: 4 feet 8 inches. The women took the skin off carefully so it can be mounted if desired.

Etah, March 22, 1914

Mene and Tauchingwa arrived at noon, deserters from the head of Bitestead Fiord. Mene wanted to turn back and did so with Mac's permission; he was not doing his share of the work. Tauchingwa left the same day without saying goodbye. We think he was afraid Mene would steal his wife, who is living here in the house with us.

Etah, March 23, 1914

Allen went on a visit to Nerky with Tauchingwa and Pooadloona. He took a stove, oil, and provisions to stay until a favorable time to return. He has kept the electric lights going all winter, and it has taken no small amount of hard work. He has made himself useful in a dozen different ways also. We see the uselessness of attempting any wireless work under the present conditions.

Ahpellah arrived with four pieces of meat and wants molasses, sugar, dog biscuits, tea, cornmeal, and oil! No trade.

Etah, March 28, 1914

I went north to Sunrise Point today and shot two eight-pound rabbits. Coming back I heard a noise on the sea ice, and looking out toward the end of the point, saw two sledges coming down off the ice foot. They proved to be Ekblaw and Kaiota. Ek left the others at the head of Bay Fiord, Ellesmere Land, all well and with plenty of game. He brought back some musk-ox skins and heads. He returned because of frostbite on the balls of both feet, which he got going up Rice Strait. He tried to continue but could not. His dog traces were in poor condition also, and the dogs were a mixture of different teams, which made it extra difficult to untangle their traces. MacMillan has given all his choice linen trace rope to the Eskimos in trade, except for his own, so that Green and Ekblaw have a poor lot of traces, weak and full of knots. Kaiota is to be given food and a sledge but not a rifle; Ek has given me these instructions from Mac.

Etah, March 31, 1914

Above zero all day today. I am going over to Hayes Sound with Freuchen and two Eskimos to put onto the shore the provisions left there on the ice.

Etah, April 16, 1914

Freuchen and I have been over and back.

Freuchen's theodolite is out of order so he is not going north this year as he had planned.

Today the ice on the inside of the attic is melting, and we are removing it in cakes, sometimes a yard square and four inches thick. Possibly a lot of this moisture came from the engine that makes our electricity.

Etah, April 20, 1914

Ek, Tank, Peter, and some Eskimos left for Umanak in the morning. If possible, Ek is to make a geological survey of the shores of Melville Bay. Tank is to stay at Umanak and do zoological work there. We will get them in the powerboat when open water comes, or Rasmussen's boat will bring them back.

Etah, April 29, 1914

Four sledges arrived from the south, and Koolatingwa wants me to go to Nerky to see his wife, who is sick. They had come up from Cape York to hunt walrus at Peteravik. She has recently had a baby.

Etah, April 30, 1914

Today I start on the 50-mile trip to Nerky with the poorest team of dogs I ever saw. Allen declares I will never get there, but I shall walk, and I have no load. Four other teams are going with me.

Nerky, May 1, 1914

My team did all right yesterday. Coming down the glacier on the southerly side of Cape Alexander, I went as fast as anyone and kept right-side up also, which two of the others did not. I saw one man come down the last sharp pitch, where one has to cut steps in order to walk down, with his sled rolling over and over. I tried to get some pictures, but the day was dark. Arrived at Nerky about five o'clock. Everybody is laughing at my team, but they pull the best they can, except one puppy who is too fat.

Koolatingwa's wife has a breast abscess, and a young baby. Just before I arrived, their daughter, about five years old, was run into by a sled and killed. They do not say much about it. I think they don't care much as the new baby is a boy. If there are several children in a family, the girls are not thought much of.

I shall wait here until the woman is better, and am living in Inyougeeto's igloo, as they have a big one and no children. They are about the best couple down here. They think a lot of each other and are as clean as necessary.

Nerky, May 4, 1914

I am in truth living off the fat of the land, or of land and water both, to be exact. I am invited to eat every little while, and as I never refuse, am in danger of bursting. I have had the first ptarmigan of the year, and rabbit, seal, and narwhal. The meat does not seem to distress me, even eaten in enormous quantities. I think I am lousy.

I lanced the abscess today and evacuated about three ounces of pus. Also I gave the mother a can of milk to feed the baby.

Peteravik, May 5, 1914

I left for home today, intending to rest the dogs overnight at Sipsoo's igloo, which is about half way. The igloo is empty, but I have made a fire in the *ikama* and cooked some seal meat. By the smell, it is a *phoca foetida*, and the meat tastes as bad as it smells. I have found enough meat for the dogs, too, and they are curled up in the snow. Snow has been falling all day, but there has been no wind.

Peteravik, Morning, May 6, 1914

When I awoke, Akkommodingwa was sitting on the bed platform eating rabbit. He had arrived sometime in the night, and without awakening me had cooked the rabbit, of which he gave me enough for a meal.

It is still snowing. Soon my visitor leaves for Nerky, and as it is lonely, I am going to at least make a start for Etah. This is the only traveling I have done alone, and I enjoy it, but am lonely as the devil.

Etah, Evening, May 6, 1914

Up over the glacier at Cape Alexander, the wind was furious and constantly blew the sled broadside to the dogs. They would not travel unless I walked in front of them. The snow was very thick, and in trying to keep sight of the Cape, I got too far over to one side and went spinning over the edge of the glacier, with the dogs following. I landed in soft snow and soon had the team going again. There was some surprise at Etah when I arrived. I was glad to get there, and the dogs were, too, especially the fat puppy. I arrived just in time for dinner.

Etah, May 19, 1914

Ahwegeea, with several others, came over the icecap today from Nerky. The sea ice is no longer safe to travel on. They want to trade, and I shall get what we need from them, giving in return tea, dog biscuit, and oil.

As everyone is free to enter the living room at any time, we never can be sure of a moment's solitude while in the house. This is according to Eskimo custom.

Etah, May 21, 1914

I have started Ooblooya and Akpoodashaho off today to meet MacMillan and Green. It is getting late, and the warm weather seems to be weakening the ice rapidly. I have given them all the available dogs and bought two for Ooblooya, so that they may have enough to supply the return party if necessary. They are to leave a cache at Pim Island in Peary's hut. I would go myself also, but dogs are not to be had.

Etah, May 22, 1914

MacMillan and Green came in today, a week earlier than we had expected. They met the two Eskimos I sent out while making camp at Payer Harbor, and with plenty of dogs, came the rest of the way on the run. Etookashoo is with them. Peeawahto died at Cape Thomas Hubbard. The men are in the best of condition but are thin. The dogs are a sad lot and have about worked themselves out. Fortunately, we have some good walrus meat for them.

Etah, May 23, 1914

MacMillan and Green, with Etookashoo and Peeawahto, went 125 miles out from Cape Thomas Hubbard and saw no land. Peary was evidently mistaken. What he saw was a mirage. They report the ice is very rough for the greater part of the way. Extreme refraction often causes rough pressure ridges of ice to resemble distant mountain peaks. There is no Crocker Land.

On the return to Cape Thomas Hubbard, Green and Peeawahto started south to find Sverdrup's record. It was while on this trip that Peeawahto was lost. I do not yet know the circumstances. MacMillan and Etookashoo had gone to Cape Colgate to get a record left by Peary. This they took, replacing it with a silk flag, their own record, and a copy of Peary's.

Etah, May 28, 1914

Jot and Panikpa are home from Anoritok, where they found plenty of seals.

We are now looking forward to my birthday and a fruitcake.

Etah, June 1, 1914

Tima [here-now]. My thirty-sixth birthday. We celebrate by eating too much.

VII

June 1 - December 31, 1914

I DISCONTINUED MY DIARY on June 1, 1914. I had come to know too many unpleasant things. There being no privacy, I could not write as I pleased.

Mac continually traded provisions and goods that had been furnished by the museum for all of us, for furs which he could sell upon return to the States. This proved to be a dangerous practice, and finally we all got together and pretty much put a stop to it. He traded sugar for foxskins so much that we feared our sugar might run low. Finally we had a meeting and voted that no more sugar would be taken on any trips except by unanimous consent.

Shortly after that Mac and I went out together. When we stopped to make tea he brought out a pound of sugar. "Have some," he said. "No, I said, "we agreed to leave all sugar at the hut for division." Another time Mac and I were out on the icepack with some Eskimos and a couple of sleds. Hunting had been poor, and we had little food for man or dog. We had agreed to share and share alike. Mac was standing aside, back to us. I had something I wanted to say to him; when I came up to him, he was eating a bar of chocolate. Things like that made me feel I was not his friend, and when he asked me I told him so. We kept our relations correct, but I found it difficult. By nature I am given to outbursts of anger, and I have always spoken my mind freely, too freely I am told, and too strongly, though I do not think so.

Mac constantly told one thing to one person and the opposite to another. He did not give the scientific men a chance to do their work. Ek fought against it and won some chances to do good work, but Tank — a different type, not a fighter — threw up his hands in disgust. They had expected to do a lot of scientific work for the University of Illinois.

When Mac and Green had been on their expedition out on the Arctic ice and had seen what they temporarily took to be the mountains of Crocker Land, it had been Peeawahto who had said no, it was mist, as it proved to be. Now Peeawahto was dead. I had come to know what had happened to him. The story we had been told that he had been killed in an avalanche was not true. Green, having no understanding whatsoever of Eskimo mentality or language, had apparently panicked and had shot him. He did not consider it murder. Peeawahto was just a savage. It was necessary that no one know of this murder so long as we were in Greenland. I would have to live with and care for a man who had killed my friend; again I found my anger hard to control, but I guess I succeeded as Green remained friendly with me. In Freuchen's book, *Peter Freuchen's Adventures in the Arctic,* he wrote that Green killed Peeawahto because he wanted Peeawahto's wife. I don't know about that.

Here is the story Green told, as given in Mac's Field Notes:

> *Monday, May 4, 1914, 55th day of the Crocker Land Trip.*
>
> A sad day for us all. It was so beautiful that I expected Fitz and Peeawahto about noon. If they did not come I had decided to go back and hunt for them. About eleven o'clock one sledge came in sight around the point above the dugout. As the other did not appear I began to fear at once that something had happened to Green. To our surprise Green appeared driving Peeawahto's sledge. He was pale and looked very much worn and tired. His first words were "Mac, this is what is left of your southern division." I said, "Good God, Green, is Peeawahto dead?"
>
> He then went on to tell me the story how they were caught in an awful blizzard fifteen miles down the coast. They made a dugout and crawled in. It was soon covered to the depth of fifteen feet; *komatiks,* dogs, everything was buried. Peeawahto refused to proceed south when it partly cleared and said he was going home. Green's dogs were never seen again. They were left under the snow, as well as the sledge. They started back with one sledge; Green's feet were freezing so he could not ride. The dogs were going so fast he could not keep up with them. Twice Peeawahto tried to get away from him, which would mean his death. He seized his rifle from the sledge and ordered Peeawahto to follow him. Looking back Green saw he was not doing so but had turned to one side. Green fired over his head first to warn him. He did not stop, so Green shot him twice, once in the body and once on the head, splitting it open. He carried the body to Cape Thomas Hubbard and left it. It is there now lying on the ground outside the door.
>
> We packed up at once as soon as we had fed him and started for home.[1]

When the truth became known after our return to the States, Green was already a war hero. I understand that Green was exonerated as having acted in self-defense, and that the Danes refrained from making a stir about it because Koodlookto, converted to Christianity, had just confessed to having killed Marvin, an American on the Peary expedition to the North Pole, also apparently in self-defense. All involved deemed it well to play down both cases.

That summer I continued my medical work with the Eskimos and the members of the expedition, and I hunted all around Etah, mostly alone. I hunted rabbits whenever I had any spare time. For a still hunter, it was a

[1]D.B. MacMillan, *Crocker Land Expedition Field Notes, No. 22.* In Rare Books and Manuscripts Room of the American Museum of Natural History, New York.

most engaging occupation. One day I turned up at the house with the hind quarters of a caribou over my shoulders, to everyone's surprise, since no one had seen a caribou so close to Etah for many years. Of course all hunting was for the table, for clothes, and for shelter. I hunted birds a lot, too, especially eider ducks. We had many shotgun cartridges, but we shot them all off, and that left us with some brass shells, maybe a hundred of them, which I would load up in the evening and the next day shoot off, bringing the ducks back to headquarters and hanging them for winter use. A little south of the duck island, but north of Etah, was a point we named Sunrise Point, because there we could first see the sun come over the horizon in the spring. At the end of the point was a high nubble with a depression behind it. Through that depression ducks would fly north and south, back and forth, in a continuous stream. There a person could shoot ducks all day long.

I set up the frame for a kayak, and the Eskimo women covered it for me with sealskins. I got many seals and walrus, first on the ice, later in the season from the kayak.

A couple of times I rowed north alone in the flattie, past Sunrise Point to Littleton Island, and camped a few days to gather eggs, about a thousand I guess. I also found a cairn with a record left by Dr. Kane, the words pricked into a piece of rough paper tucked into a cap lining. It said, "All well, Kane, Aug. 29-53. [1853] Gone south." It had kept perfectly for 61 years!

Once, a herd of walrus came up around me, and they were too interested in my little boat. Their whiskered faces and shining white tusks kept popping out of the blue water everywhere. I think they were just curious, but I would be no match for a ton of walrus, so I banged the oars on the boat and yelled as loud as I could, and off they went. If I had shot one, the others might have ganged up on me. We went after them later with the whaleboat. Jot and I shot a big one dead, Nookapingwa got a harpoon into him, and we cut him up on a big ice floe. While we were enjoying the clams he had shucked for us, I looked up, and there was an iceberg in the grip of tide and wind coming at us like a ship under power. We moved away fast, but a thick fog came in, and we got caught in the ice floes swirling around in the heavy tide. Our rudder was smashed to smithereens before we managed to get into a little cove out of the clutch of the moving ice. When the tide changed and cleared a lead of open water for us, the fog lifted and we headed home.

In the autumn, needing skins and meat for the winter, the Etah Eskimos went hunting caribou 50 miles or so north. At this time of year, the coast was bare of snow and ice, so they used the icecap as a road for their sledges. To get up on the icecap, they climbed Brother John's Glacier, at the head of Foulke Fiord.

At Borup Lodge we needed skins and meat too, so on September 11, 1914, I went on my first caribou hunt. I ferried all my gear by motorboat to the head of the fiord and portaged it up the brook and past Alida Lake to where the glacier comes down. We had a dinner of walrus meat, crackers, and tea. I cut steps in the face of the glacier till nine p.m. Akpoodashaho was with me. Panikpa, Kakotcheea, and Ahnowka were along. I guess we were about a dozen, with women to sew and cook for us. We had a quiet night at the foot of the glacier, but the next day it was blowing and snowing. Panikpa's *tupik* blew down. The strong wind prevented going on the icecap, so I returned to Etah for the night. I was up at four a.m., had breakfast, and kayaked to the head of the fiord, blown along by a west wind. I found the Eskimos in bed. We hauled the dogs and sledges up the face of the glacier on lines and drove along the edge of the icecap with good going and the dogs on the jump all day. We pitched the tents at nine p.m., had grub, and slept till seven in the morning.

That day we came down off the icecap and pitched our tents about five or six miles from it, where a brook came down from underneath the ice, and we hunted. We saw no tracks, so we traveled along for about three more days, looking for signs of caribou. We got some ptarmigan and rabbits, which I cooked, and finally we shot three *tuctu* (caribou). My ship biscuits were all gone, since Ahnowka and Akpoodashaho were with me, and do they like biscuits! I had thought I could live exclusively on the Eskimo diet of meat, but the attempt was not a success. I had plenty of caribou meat, but found I could not keep up my strength and did not feel well. It is true that I was traveling every day and working hard, but I did suffer from lack of carbohydrates. I lost twenty pounds, and gained back fifteen in three days when I returned to Etah.

It had been snowing pretty steadily, but finally it stopped. We left the *tupiks* standing, went hunting, and found plenty of tracks. The hunting was good, so we hunted in this area for, I guess, about a week.

A Polar Inuit cannot get married until he has shot a caribou, so Ahnowka had borrowed a rifle to shoot his first caribou. There were five tents on the right-hand side of a brook. A big buck caribou stood on the opposite side, watching us. We left the dogs with the women. We walked quietly toward him with soft boots in single file with our rifles on our shoulders. The idea was to make him think we were caribou. I think he had never seen a man before. There were ten or eleven of us, and we walked to within about fifty or sixty yards from him. They urged me to shoot, but I said, "No, let Ahnowka shoot him." He was a tall, slender, and good boy, though not as good a companion as was young Kakotcheea the following year. He shot the caribou in the neck, killing him with only one shot. Now Ahnowka could get married.

Once in a while there comes a terrific wind from the icecap, where Torngak, the devil, lives. It struck us once this trip. I was in my tent. I got out and walked around and around the tent, wrapping it with a sealskin line. The wind was so strong it blew me onto my back several times. I had to crawl on my hands and knees to carry rocks to hold the tent down. There were about six inches of soft snow, and in less than an hour all that snow had gone. Ahnowka's mother was in a small tent not far away, and it blew down. She was walking in circles in a peculiar kind of fit, a *piblockto,* so called, a sort of hysteria the Eskimos have. I saw Akpoodashaho's wife trying to make a flame with caribou tallow. She could not melt it and was chewing it up and spitting it out into her *ikama*. I took my primus stove over to melt it for her and get her fire started.

On that trip we were gone 15 days and got 42 fine skins and all the meat we could carry. We came back with the best-fed dogs you ever saw.

We enlivened the dark month of December by putting on a show for the Eskimos. We had magic tricks, a chorus line, and I performed an operation on Jot. His head stuck up through a hole in the table at the end of a sheet-covered dummy, which the Eskimos all believed was firmly attached to his grinning head. Howls of laughter followed screams of horror as I sliced into his stomach with a butcher knife and produced various oddments such as a hunk of meat, fur, a string of popcorn, and triumphantly, a life-sized baby doll. I then decapitated my victim, tossed his body to the audience, and brought down the house, almost literally.

On the day before Christmas, with a new moon to light their way, Mac and Tank left for Umanak and points south with the mail and our request for a relief ship the following summer.

ETAH
November 3, 1914

My dearest Marion:

There is a chance that Mac may get to Upernavik with the mail sometime before Christmas. We were sorry not to get mail off on Rasmussen's ship in the summer, but ice conditions made it impossible for them to get here. They sent their mail from Umanak by motor boat under very adverse conditions. Our boat was walrus hunting about thirty miles south of Etah and by good luck met them, whereupon they transferred what mail they had, and Rasmussen's boat headed south immediately. Ekblaw was there and scribbled the few lines he had time to write.

I believe that, owing to the slip-up in the mail last summer, the Museum may not have been definitely informed that we want a ship sent to take us home next summer. We now expect them to receive word in May, which does not leave them much time to get a ship started up here. They may hire Rasmussen's ship to fetch us, in which case we would go to Denmark. I have a very cordial letter from Rasmussen in the last mail. The other ship which we expected did not get north of Upernavik, so far as we have heard.

The plans are made for trips next spring. I am not going on any of the long ones; I was given a chance to go, but it would be unnecessary. I hope that, knowing this, you will not worry. There are no real dangers, but I am taking no chances of not getting back to you and Ruth. I am too selfish.

Last summer we spent at Etah, making trips for game when the ice permitted, and to Littleton Island after eider ducks and eggs. I made two trips there, once in the whaleboat, which has since been lost in the ice, and once in the rowboat, which holds only one comfortably. I think we have several thousand eggs and about fifty walrus.

This fall I went north over the icecap about fifty miles, caribou hunting. We got forty-two in two weeks.

Allen and Green have built a hut on an island at the mouth of the harbor and installed the wireless there. They are trying to get up the wire by means of kites, but with poor success so far. The whole outfit is far too small. Allen is a worker and a fine fellow, and is very much put out. Green is pleasure loving, and so long as he is comfortable, doesn't care. He likes sledging trips, however, and is very useful because of his ability to take correct observations.

By the way, I am afraid Peary is in for some hard knocks, as he well deserves to be. Peary Channel, which he discovered, does not exist. He did not explore far enough to find out it was only a bay. Crocker Land does not exist either.

I can take observations for latitude and do coast survey work to some extent. The compass needle here points about southwest instead of north and is very confusing. Ek and I recently found the altitude of the highest hill near the house to be 1800 feet. I shot two caribou near there in the summer at a distance of 380 yards, which is good shooting.

All the party are in good health, and most of us heavier than usual. I lost 20 pounds on the caribou trip, weighing less than 160 when I got back, but am 186 now.

I hope nothing of mine will get into the papers. Hovey prints whatever he gets hold of. He wrote to Green's father for a letter, saying he would not publish it, but he did, so don't let him fool you. I am sending you some personal pictures. I really look better than they show. I was very thankful for those you sent me. They are a comfort to me. There have been times I pretty near started to walk home.

We expect to get to New York late in September. I am afraid it may be too cold at Islesboro, and probably Ruth will be going to school by that time, so you do whatever it seems best at the time. I think we will be rather short of funds. If your people need you, stay with them, surely, and I will come to you. I only hope they are both there to need you.

I should like to study some when I get back. I should also wish to make a home where we could take proper care of your father and mother. I do not see much of an opening in Bangor, with Father and Barb [Hal's sister] already doctors there. It would be slow at first anyway, but may be all right in the long run. I think you had better decide; I admit my incompetence to do so.

Every night I go to sleep wishing you were beside me. I am never really contented or happy without you. With you, even if we have no more children, I shall be content. I know we both want more, however, and I hope it will be a boy.

We miss a bath up here as much as we do any civilized convenience. Our tub has not been used for nearly a year now. No one seems to want to heat enough water to fill it, which would be difficult in winter anyway. I think I am the cleanest, but the others dispute it. I found one louse on my undershirt today, the first for a long time. Allen is terribly afraid of taking them home with him. I think our things will have to be fumigated at New York. Probably I shall need to stop there two or three days after getting back, to settle with the Museum and to see about the use of the pictures. Then can we not have a few quiet days together somewhere? Probably not. Anyway, if you are near I shall be happy.

I may bring my kayak home unless I wear it out next summer. I built it last spring, and the Eskimo women sewed on the sealskin cover for me. They last only about two seasons. I am a fair kayaker, but I take no chances.

I have done nothing about the position offered me as doctor at Upernavik and shall not, although it will be open to me at any time. I don't know that I want to be hogtied to business in a city, but guess that is what it will come to in the end.

I ask your forgiveness for going on this trip. It was thoughtlessness. I want to get back now much more than I wanted to go then.

I am on watch tonight and am cook for the two meals tomorrow. It is two in the morning now, and I have baked one strawberry and four mince pies, besides putting two pots of beans in to bake. I am in charge of the meat room and have a lot of meat hung on nails: seal, walrus, rabbit, caribou, ducks, and ptarmigan. It stays frozen all year. We have eggs twice a week. Our canned fruits are fine and in great plenty: peaches, pears, plums, and cherries. Our food is excellent, and thanks to your training, I am an excellent cook. Jot is not an extra good cook, so we are glad to take turns.

Our harbor is frozen solid. All last winter we did not have half the snow that we did at Island Falls, and most of that blew away. Lord knows we have wind enough. We try to get out every day for exercise, but the days are short, and one cannot see well to shoot a rifle even at noon. At night we play cribbage, poker, and chess. Then we read a little, go to bed, and dream of home.

With all my love and devotion,

Hal Hunt

HEADQUARTERS
CROCKER LAND EXPEDITION
December 20, 1914

Dear Mrs. Hunt:

This is just a line to add, if possible, a very tiny bit to the happiness I know this day must hold for you with Hal's letters in your hand.

Your man is as fat as butter, while I am thinner than skimmed milk. Our temperaments must make the difference, for we are living like kings.

Hal tells us of his home when we ask him. He never descends to moody expressions of loneliness or longing. But I would have you know that, in spite of his reserve, no man has ever made me feel so strongly the richness of life that can come with such as he possesses: a fortune which seems boundless, consisting of you and Ruth. For the first time in my life, I have come to realize that a wife, if of the right kind, must be far beyond any success or fame, for she combines the very satisfaction of both.

You should be happy!

Sincerely,
Fitzhugh Green

Doctor Hunt in Etah, Greenland.

Above left: Etookshoo and a wolf. Above right: Borup Lodge, Etah.
Below: Ahnahwe making thread at sunrise point.

Above left: Akpoodashaho with a harpoon of narwhal horn. Above right: Nelleka with white and blue fox. Below: Nellekateeah and Nelleka chewing skins to soften them.

Above: Working on a narrow ice foot at Cape Sabine, Ellesmere Land. Below: Crossing from ice cakes to shore in the spring at Etah.

Above: Exploring an iceberg off Etah. Below: The *Cluett* in the ice off Cape York.

Above: Dogs harnessed to a sledge. Below: Dinner at Etah, December 13, 1914. Photo taken by D.B. MacMillan.

VIII

Winter and Spring, 1915

During the winter of 1915, Allen and Green were sick, Tank froze his toes, and I had a toothache. Now a toothache doesn't sound like much, but this one was monumental.

When I was in college, playing football for Bowdoin, a Yale man had given me an illegal punch on the jaw, injuring a wisdom tooth. At Etah, the tooth began to ache. I got a pair of tooth forceps and asked the man on watch to put the forceps on the tooth, pull hard, and pull the tooth out. He got the forceps on the tooth, and then his courage failed him. He took them off again without pulling, which left me with the toothache.

The next day — this was, mind you, in the middle of the winter, very cold — Kakotcheea, Ahnowka, and I started for Peter Freuchen's place at Umanak. I knew Peter had tooth forceps and had had some medical training, so he could pull the tooth. It took us five days to reach him. That tooth caused me a lot of misery on the way. With every breath I took, the cold came right on the sore tooth. I had some morphine pills, and when I couldn't stand it any more I would pop a pill under my tongue. When I was too much under the morphine, I would tell the Eskimos I was tired, and I would crawl into my sleeping bag and go to sleep on the sled. The two men didn't have much equipment, so they would build a snow house for shelter — not a good one, but one they could crawl into.

One day on the way the visibility was zero, and we got lost cutting across a deep bay on the sea ice. Even in the middle of the winter, the ice on the sea was always moving, driven by winds and currents. It built up sharp pressure ridges, then jumbled them all together, or suddenly split apart, making a lead of open water with steamy Arctic smoke hanging over the break in the ice. Blindly we worked our way up and over hill after hill of rough, broken ice and snow; the dogs' traces became hopelessly tangled time and again; and time and again we had to detour around leads, which loomed suddenly dark in the whiteout, almost at our feet. After many hours of this, my tooth aching something wicked, we found ourselves back at our starting place. Kakotcheea shrugged his shoulders and said: "This time we go along the edge of the coast and we get there."

Just as I was walking up to Peter's front door, the tooth stopped aching, and it never ached again. Nonetheless, when I returned to civilization I had to have all my teeth extracted. In those four years, they had deteriorated surprisingly, though causing no more pain. I also gradually became hard of hearing, most likely due to repeated exposure to wind and extreme weather while sick with colds and the flu. Being the only doctor and dentist had its disadvantages.

Peter didn't have much to eat; his ordinary civilized food was all gone. He had some birds he had caught in the summer, and they were very strong. I had no desire to eat rotten meat, but I was hungry, and pretty soon I began to relish those birds. Still, we didn't stay any longer than we had to.

Early in February it must have been — it was still pretty dark — we heard that the Eskimos in Peteravik were sick with the flu, so I went to see if I could help. Every time the mailboat or sledge came to North Greenland, it brought disease: mumps, flu, whatever, as well as mail. The Eskimos were the sickest of all. Never having been exposed, they hadn't built up resistance to these illnesses.

An unusually high tide had jammed rough ice up over the ice foot, which made the going awful. It was a long haul. When we got there I was dreadfully tired. Everyone was asleep. I had to drive the dogs out of the narrow entrance to Sipsoo's igloo before I could crawl in, and then I hurried, as I didn't want my pants bitten at the seat. The family was sleeping on the narrow shelf at the back of the igloo. I lay down next to the wall, as far as possible from the children, so in the night they would not get all over me, for believe me, they did not smell sweet. I had a terrific headache and was homesick. I got up and sat by the smoky *ikama* with my head in my hands. Sipsoo awoke and saw me. Without a word, he got up, cut some frozen meat, cooked it, and left it by my side. He did not offer it to me, as it might embarrass me if I had to refuse.

I found the flu had run its course, and they had plenty of meat. We came home in a few days.

Upon my return, I found Green deteriorating mentally and physically. He was in a difficult position, and I feared a nervous breakdown. He was not taking care of himself. With Mac's backing, I prescribed a strict regimen of regular meals, exercise, work, and sleep, and saw to it that he followed it. He gradually improved.

Tank came back from the mail trip to the south with both big toes frozen. The traveling must have been agony for him, but he never complained. He would not let me amputate immediately, as should have been done. I think he hoped to save the toes. As a result, he suffered bravely but unnecessarily until he consented to an operation. Afterwards, because of the delay, healing was slow.

That spring Ekblaw made a most admirable trip with two Eskimos across Ellesmere Land, into Greely Fiord. He mapped hitherto undiscovered fiords and found a pass connecting Greely Fiord with Lake Hazen, through which they went onward to Fort Conger. Thence they sledged down Kennedy Channel, Kane Basin, and Smith Sound to Etah. Remains of long-unused Eskimo winter houses were found all along this route, thus establishing it as the ancient Eskimo road to Greenland from the west. He did valuable work in geology and mineralogy. Bear, seal, and musk oxen were abundant. The party cached their pemmican and subsisted mainly on game as they went along. The dogs reveled in musk-ox meat.

Towards the end of March, Mac and I went to Sulwuddy and Peteravik for seal and walrus. Where six weeks earlier there had been plenty to eat, now game was scarce. Hoping for walrus, about 30 Eskimos, again bringing sickness with them, had arrived from their homes to the south; both they and their dogs were nearly starving. Every spring at this time, the Polar Inuit gathered there, driven by hunger, to hunt walrus and seal at their blow holes and along leads and the edge of the open sea. The sun already was above the horizon at noon. Usually it was an annual picnic, a gathering of old friends after the winter. Usually walrus and seal came out on the ice in this area in great numbers. This time these sick men with their thin dogs headed out toward the sea over the ice fields every morning, to return at night, most often empty handed, though sometimes joyously pulling a seal or a 1,000-pound walrus. Sometimes leads of water opened up between hunter and shore. Sometimes the ice was so thin that it bent under the sledges, or it was so rotten that the sledge runners made tracks of slush. For several days there was a strong offshore wind, and danger of being carried out to sea on an ice pan kept the Eskimos ashore.

After a while the hunting got better, and we could go home with well-fed dogs and good loads of meat. The sleds were heavy, so I left Mac to ride the sled with the Eskimos, and I walked the 25 miles home alone. I spent the night in Sulwuddy. It was a pleasant walk.

That winter at Etah we had so much company, so many Eskimos with their dog teams, that they gradually ate up our accumulated dog food. It was therefore suggested that one Eskimo and I take all available dogs to Ellesmere Land and live off the country, bringing back what skins we could. This I was glad to hear, and my friend, Akpoodashaho, was delighted also.

> Do you know the long day's patience, belly-down on frozen drift,
> While the head of heads is feeding out of range?
> It is there that I am going, where the boulders and the snow lie,
> With a trusty, nimble tracker that I know.

We corralled all the dogs we could find; finally he had 23 and I had 10. We fed them so they would be strong; we got our hunting equipment together; and we started.

We left about April twenty-first. The first day was north along the Greenland shore to Anoritok. My dogs spent that day getting acquainted with each other, and I had to train them to pull together. I had nine female dogs in my team. They were fighting all the time among themselves because no one dog could gain predominance. In the beginning, some were lazy and would stop if I turned to speak to Akpoodashaho. I had one that was an awful loafer, so I tied a knot in her trace, keeping her within reach, and every time she slackened I touched her with the whip. Finally she learned I meant business, and I let out her trace. She pulled like a good one all the rest of the way. Once, going up a rise, I was pushing all I could, and one of the dogs turned, looked around, and lay down. I went toward her with the whip. Before I came to her, she got up and began to pull; in fact, they all began to pull and went up the hill with a rush. I didn't need to push at all, and I had been pushing my heart out to help them. When I came back to Etah, they were all pulling together splendidly.

Akpoodashaho, when he came to a rise, would scold his dogs and then go in back of the sledge and push. His dogs would lie down on him. Then he would go forward and whip. They would pull a little and then stop to see what he would do. He had the strongest team, and when chasing a bear, his team would beat mine all to pieces, because they wanted to go. But I could beat him on the trail.

The second day we crossed Smith Sound to Pim Island, off the coast of Ellesmere Land, a 27-mile trip. There we slept and fed the dogs on some walrus meat we found frozen in the ice. Digging it out, I broke the pickax handle. Opening a coffin for wood, I struck my knee on a nail and was lamed. On account of my knee and a strong wind, we spent a few days in Peary's old hut there, as there was plenty of dog food and fuel for the stove. There was some coal about. If you hunted for it for half an hour, you could get a hatful, mixed maybe with a few rocks. On about the fifth day of the trip, we went to the end of Flagler Fiord, which bites into Ellesmere Land a long way, some say 50 miles. We spent the night in a large snow igloo Akpoodashaho had built the previous year near a cache of pemmican. Our sledging diet of half a pound of pemmican each, with hard bread, tea, and condensed milk night and morning, proved sufficient. When frozen, the pemmican was as hard as a rock and had to be attacked with a hatchet. I usually dropped my chunk into hot tea and took them mixed. We found tea better than coffee. With coffee at dinner, we often had to leave our warm sleeping bags to urinate after a few hours, and with tea we did not. The dogs had a pound of dog pemmican at the end of each day's work, although we fed them fresh meat when possible. A steady diet of pemmican gave them diarrhea from too much salt.

The following day we climed the icecap of Ellesmere Land. The weather was fine, traveling was good, and the dogs seemed to enjoy it, so we kept going for 24 hours and went all the way across, without stopping, to Bay Fiord, on the western shore of Ellesmere Land. There we pitched our tent and rested two nights, and there Akpoodashaho shot a seal, which we fed to both the dogs and ourselves.

When we were rested, we packed up and went searching with our binoculars for bear out on the ice of Bay Fiord and for musk oxen and caribou along the shore. It was a beautiful sunny day with no wind, and the surface of the ice was pretty well covered with bear tracks. At that time of year, seals were pupping, and bears were hunting all over for evidence of young ones. The small harbor seals, which polar bear live off in winter, keep air holes open through the ice, and in the spring they enlarge an air hole up into a drift of snow, and there the pups are born. The bear walks along from drift to drift. When he smells seal, he rears up on his hind legs, pounces down to break the crust, and grabs the young seal with his left paw. He eats only the fat and buries the rest to eat later, whenever he may need it. In the stomach of a bear, we usually found several quarts of liquid oil with a little skin and hair mixed in with it.

We finally saw a bear; Akpoodashaho saw him first. We took our loads off the sledges and advanced toward the bear slowly. A bear can run fast for great distances, and without dogs, a hunter has no chance to catch up with him. Dogs make the bear stop and defend himself, so one can come close enough to shoot. Our dogs had not seen this one yet, and the bear had not been aware we were coming. When we got within about 200 yards, the bear heard us. He looked up. So many dogs coming scared him, and he started to run toward an iceberg. We cut the dogs loose, thinking they would surround him and stop him, but he arrived at the iceberg at the same time the dogs did. The bear and dogs disappeared behind the berg. In a second they all reappeared running around together on the top. One dog was knocked off the steep side of the berg, fell at our feet, and was killed. The bear, chasing him, fell partway over but hung on by his elbows and front claws. He looked down at us right below him and slowly dropped on his haunches about ten yards from us. He turned and growled and then shuffled off around the berg to where there was a chance to climb it. I was trying to take a picture, but Akpoodashaho urged me to shoot him, because he would probably kill some more dogs, so I shot him dead, in the neck. He rolled over and over down to the ground, and the dogs came around and chewed at him. I told Akpoodashaho they would spoil the skin, but he said they couldn't put a tooth through it. Finally we pulled the dogs loose, tied them up, skinned the bear, fed the dogs, and ate all we could ourselves; the meat was raw, warm, and steaming in the cold. Then I pitched my tent, unrolled my sleeping bag, got inside, and went to sleep.

Akpoodashaho climbed the berg with the glasses. He came down, shook me, and said: "*Nagorsakswa,* I see more bear." "I think they aren't bear," I said, "They must be wolves." "No," he said, "I know a bear when I see one." I got out of the sleeping bag, put my clothes on, and hitched up my dogs. It proved to be a mother bear with two half-grown year-old cubs. These would make good museum specimens, so we carefully shot them, skinned them, and saved the leg bones and skulls. Then we went back to our tent and slept.

The next morning we started out again bear hunting. We traveled maybe an hour or two. Akpoodashaho had the glasses, and at every elevation he climbed up on it to look around. Finally he came to me and said: "*Nagorsakswa,* I think I saw a bear, but it didn't move so I guess it is just a lump of ice." He kept looking over in that direction, and pretty soon he said: "I saw it move." We dumped our loads and went after him. It proved to be an extremely large bear, watching by a seal hole, very much as a cat stands by a mouse hole, and that is why he hadn't been moving.

We cut the dogs loose, and he saw us coming. He moved away at a walking pace, but, being such a large bear, his walk was about as fast as our run, and we could not catch up with him. When the dogs surrounded him, he started running, taking about 20 feet at each step. Akpoodashaho said, "Oh, we have lost the bear and our dogs, too." I felt a bullet go by my ear and heard him shoot. I looked back, and there was Akpoodashaho kneeling down shooting. I was right in line between him and the bear. That bullet must have hit the bear, which made him think one of the dogs had bitten him, because he stopped and began to fight them, so we did not have to run any more. When we came up to the bear, I shot him and broke his neck.

The bear was so big that when we had skinned out one side we had difficulty pulling him over to skin out the other. We got a very fine skin. We pulled it out, straightened it, and trampled it flat so it would go well on the sled. Then we buried it in the snow and started to go on, thinking we might see another bear, but there was a chill north wind, we were tired, and the dogs were full of meat. We picked up the bearskin, sidled up to an iceberg that gave us shelter from the wind, and pitched our tent, just north of a large island off the mouth of Bay Fiord.

The polar bear has never had anything to fear in the Arctic. No other animal can attack him successfully; therefore, he travels wherever he wants to, usually alone. One summer day, a bear came swimming into Foulke Fiord, right by our house, and he let the men get quite close to him, so Mac got some fine pictures. He is as at home in the water as on land. Once a baby polar bear followed his mother's skin into Etah and stayed for weeks. He had his favorites, especially one little Eskimo boy, whom he would follow about like a Newfoundland dog. They went sliding together down a big bank behind the house. He could not be tied up and did about as he pleased.

A polar bear will not ordinarily attack a man, but if he were hungry, as they are sometimes in the middle of winter, he would probably kill a man to eat him. Several times I have been warned not to go off alone without a rifle, because a bear might be hungry and tackle me. The polar bear is probably the second largest carnivorous animal in the world.

Once when I went to see a wounded Eskimo I was out walking alone in the dusk near the village. I saw a lump of snow that moved, so I knew it was a bear. I started back toward the village, and the bear was after me. I ran as fast as I could. I could almost feel the breath of that bear down the back of my neck. Before I came to the Eskimo igloos, a few stray dogs found us and bothered the bear enough to cover my retreat. Actually, I know of no bear having attacked a man, but it could happen. Looking back, I can see I was very foolish to travel alone without a rifle.

Akpoodashaho did not let me sleep very long. Pretty soon he was shaking me again and saying he saw some musk oxen. I thought they were rocks, but he said he had seen them move. We now had five bear skins, all we wanted, but we did want some musk-ox skins for sleeping bags and igloo platforms.

Provided he has a few companions, the musk ox, like the bear, travels without fear of any other animal. One musk ox can be killed by a wolf, but when the musk oxen are together, they stand back to back with their heads out. They have thick, heavy skulls, big horns, and sharp hooves. Neither a bear nor wolves will attack them. They are easily killed with a rifle, because they will stand there, not moving, until the last one is killed. Once when I was shooting musk oxen, a bull started to charge. I let fly at his head, and he only backed up a little. I shot him through the neck, and he dropped as if struck by lightning.

Akpoodashaho and I left our tent and load out by the berg and started after the herd. The land was uneven, and my dogs got all caught up in their traces so I cut them loose. Akpoodashaho turned his sled over, so his dogs could not drag it, and left dogs and sledge while we went up to the herd of ten musk oxen, which my dogs had surrounded. When they had seen us coming, they had run away about a quarter of a mile onto the top of a hill, where they formed their defensive circle, heads out, but they had left a small calf behind. Before I could get to him, my dogs had mauled him. I kicked them away, they ran after the herd, and I picked up the little musk ox, only a week or so old, and put him on his feet. He didn't seem injured. There was no blood on him, his skin was not torn, and he could stand, but when I came back to him in about an hour he was dead. Because we needed the meat and skins, we killed all ten musk oxen and took the calf's skin too.

About halfway back to the tent, I saw what looked to be a stray dog. It came to me that it must not be a dog but a wolf. I stopped my dogs, took careful aim, and shot. When I went over to see him, he lay on the snow without a sign of blood on him. I thought he was just stunned and might get up and grab me, so I poked him cautiously with the rifle until I finally made up my mind he was really dead. I had shot him through the eye. I hung him inside the tent from the tent pole, as I did not want him to freeze before Akpoodashaho skinned him. From the top of the tent pole where I hitched his feet, his nose touched the ground. He was a remarkably good specimen.

Pretty soon Akpoodashaho came back. He peeked into the tent and said, "*Now-i-o!* That is a very big rabbit!"

Arctic wolves are rare animals and do not roam in packs as wolves do down south. They are relatives to the Eskimo dogs, who are inclined to be rather friendly with them. They are white, almost as white as the bear, with a few iron-grey hairs on the back of their necks and along their spines. They stand tall, and their heads are enormous.

Besides our own outfit we now had five bear skins, ten musk-ox skins, the white wolf, and bones for mounting specimens at the Museum. A heavy load. Some days later, we shot five more musk oxen, and then we had all the skins we could handle. It was time to start for Etah. We packed up our sleds, laid the skins as flat as we could on them, and headed back for the head of Bay Fiord, where we camped that night. The next day we started up over the icecap from Bay Fiord to Flagler Fiord. With such heavy loads, we had to double-track.

The dogs were so tired we decided to camp right on the icecap that night, though we had no dog food because of the heavy loads. As soon as we got down to land at Flagler Fiord, we shot about a dozen rabbits, chopped them in two, and gave each dog half a rabbit. They ate everything: skin, hair, bones, and all.

On the way home we stayed at Peary's old hut on Pim Island again and chopped plenty of meat for all concerned from that walrus we had found frozen in the ice. The crossing of Smith Sound went well, and we stayed at Anoritok in an old snow house. Going south to Etah we found soft ice on the sea and had to go inland, up the face of the steep peninsula and down the precipitous drop behind Borup Lodge. The dogs were tired and the snow was soft, so we dumped our loads about six miles out of camp, to send back for them the next day. When we asked the men to get them for us, they were a bit peeved, but when they brought them back they said, "We don't wonder you dropped them. What a load for two dog teams!" It seems to me it was a pile as big as this room when we unloaded. We had been gone a little over three weeks. While I did not become fluent in the Eskimo's complicated language, I knew the working words and never had any communication problem in all that time with Akpoodashaho, nor later with other Polar Inuit.

Akpoodashaho and I had had such a successful trip and were so happy he told me: "*Nagorsakswa, Nanookswa,* you and I are brothers." About a month later, he came to me with a fine musk-ox sleeping bag that his wife had made for me.

IX

June, 1915 - December 1916 The Relief Ships Are Frozen In

DURING THE SUMMER OF 1915 we packed and prepared for the arrival of our relief ship. I had my medical duties and whenever possible went hunting for the pot. That summer I had a real tub bath, hot too. All the water for the house had to be hauled up, often in the form of ice from a berg, so we used it sparingly. In June we took our water tank over to the brook, filled it, lit a fire under it, and took turns in it. Luxury!

The sun rolled around the horizon hour after hour and slipped out of sight for a longer period each day. The middle of August came, and still no ship. We checked our stores and found we were low in some items; Mac had still been trading for furs. We chose a committee to ration our provisions from then on. I made no bones about how upset I was, and Mac didn't like it. Tank, Ek, Green, and Allen got together and decided they would appoint me leader of the expedition if Mac did not go along. I think Mac never knew about this. According to our contract with the Museum, this was mutiny they were discussing. We had signed the document that stated that "MacMillan is the sole leader of the expedition, . . . his authority is to be recognized at all times and full obedience accorded to his orders, . . . insubordination, disobedience or incompetence may be punished by suspension or expulsion from the staff, the salary or salaries of the man or men affected being withheld . . ."

We knew we must get meat for the winter. We rowed and paddled south, through the windy chop off Cape Alexander, to the walrus- and seal-hunting grounds at Sulwuddy. We had good hunting, brought all the meat we could carry back to headquarters, and cached some tons of walrus at Sulwuddy for winter use. Back at Etah, we lugged tons of coal in boats from Provision Point to the house, and then I went north caribou hunting. We had given up hope for a ship.

MacMillan suggested I take along Kakotcheea, younger brother of

Etookashoo, and son of Panikpa. I guess he was about 18 years old, not married, an intelligent, fairly strong young man. He was more than willing to go with me, and had equipment from Etookashoo: a musk-ox sleeping bag, foot gear, and clothing. I had that fine musk-ox bag Akpoodashaho had given me and was very glad of it. When you first get into a musk-ox bag, it is cold, like cold sheets, whereas a caribou bag is like woolen blankets, but the musk-ox bag is by far the best in really cold weather. We went up on the icecap and sledged north about 50 miles or more. Wind on the icecap can stir up snow so it is apparently snowing, and when the wind starts the snow drifting that way, it is a rather serious condition. One of those storms caught us up there. I knew what I wanted to do but asked Kakotcheea what he thought. He said I should decide. He felt I knew as well as he did or better.

I had been there the year before. I told him I thought I knew where we were, and we could drift downhill onto the land to get out of the wind. He said that would be fine, so we did, he flipping his whiplash back and forth in front of the dogs so they would not go too fast, and I holding back on the sled upstanders so the sled would not overrun the dogs. The downhill slope was not excessive, and we made it to the land, about two miles, without any difficulty. We turned right about half a mile until we came to a bay in the icecap where there was no wind. There we made the dogs fast, fed them, pitched our tent, and went to sleep. In the middle of the night there was a furious wind from the opposite direction, and the tent began to slat. I reached out of my bag and pulled at the lower end of the tent pole, letting the tent fall onto us. We rolled the tent around us and went to sleep again. When we next awoke it was all quiet.

We crawled out of the tent, put on our clothing, and had breakfast. I told Kakotcheea I would go hunting, and when he was ready he could hitch up the dogs and follow. We were beside one of the many small brooks coming out from underneath the icecap. I walked down the brook, so Kakotcheea would have no trouble finding me. I walked along for three or four miles and, looking back for Kakotcheea, saw the antlers of two buck caribou coming along right where I had expected to see him. I lay down behind a snow drift, waited for them to come within 50 yards, and shot them. Kakotcheea came with the dogs. We cleaned the caribou, fed the dogs, ate what meat we could, and camped right there. The next morning although, since I was already growing deaf, I could not hear them, he told me he could hear voices not far away, so we broke camp and joined some other Eskimos also hunting caribou.

Kakotcheea was such an intelligent young man that I had taught him to figure. He knew English but would not speak it. One day I came back very late from hunting alone to find him sitting up in his sleeping bag with a pencil and paper figuring. I said: "Why don't you go to sleep?" and he answered: "*Nagorsakswa* was gone a long time, and I was a little bit worried." He was that kind of a man, careful of his companion.

When we had 20 skins, we added what meat we could carry, cached the rest, and went back onto the icecap. Pushing the loaded sledge up the icecap, I apparently strained my heart, because I had shortness of breath and my ankles swelled for a few weeks. I paid no attention to it, and eventually the condition disappeared. At Brother John's Glacier at the head of Foulke Fiord we found that the steps we had cut had filled up. I asked Kakotcheea what we should do, but he again wanted me to decide. I said we should slide down. He smiled. It was not very far, maybe 20 or 30 feet, but we could not see what we would land on, soft snow or rocks. We whipped the dogs back so they would hold us back a little, and down we went over the edge. We landed, dogs, sled, Kakotcheea, and I, all in a mess, on soft snow. Fortunately, the dogs were friendly. After we got straightened out, I left him with everything to look for my kayak, which had been left for me at the water's edge. The fiord is about two miles long, and the walking was very poor. From where I left Kakotcheea to the edge of the water was about half a mile. The light was poor, the kayak had been weighted down with rocks, and it was some time before I stumbled on it.

I put the kayak in the water and climbed in. The wind was blowing viciously down the fiord, so that I had to backpaddle all the way to keep from going too fast. The shore was lined with rocks and reefs, and the wind stirred up the water into a constant froth. As I came to headquarters, I had to turn, and there the waves began to come in, because I did not have on the kayak costume. I paddled hurriedly to reach the shore, and just as I arrived I heard a yell.

The door burst open, and many Eskimos poured out, came down to the shore, and lifted me, kayak and all, out of the water. They asked where Kakotcheea was, and I told them he was all right. Mac came to greet me, and he said: "They've all gone. Just you, Jot, and I remain." The relief ship, the *George B. Cluett,* had come and gone. It had only been able to reach North Star Bay (Umanak). Freuchen had come to Etah in his powerboat to pick up our party for the trip home.

The next day we attempted to go up the fiord in the whaleboat after Kakotcheea. It was blowing so hard that even with six oars the boat was blown right astern. We had to wait another day for the wind to calm down. When it did, and we went up and found Kakotcheea, he was smiling as usual, and we took him, the dogs, sleds, and skins in the whaleboat back to headquarters.

I felt pretty low and lonely. Mac and Jot stayed by choice, but I had had enough of that expedition, and particularly of Mac. I was like a caged animal. When Mac said I could go south the next spring, I immediately brought out my suitcase! Then I came down with one of my migraine headaches. I learned later that if Mac and Jot had not chosen to stay, Ek would have stayed for my sake — and he had a fiancee waiting for him. That is friendship.

We were kept busy getting ready for the winter. Later, when ice formed, I walked all over Foulke Fiord and made holes in the ice, much as you would make ice-fishing holes, to make soundings, which had never been done. The fiord was very deep, having been scoured out by the glacier. Mac went south to pick up provisions left by the *Cluett*, only to come back with the news that the *Cluett* was frozen in at Parker Snow Bay, halfway between North Star Bay and Cape York, and was itself in need of provisions and a doctor.

As soon as I could, I left with three sledges for Parker Snow Bay. That was in November of 1915. I never went back to Etah afterwards. I lived on shipboard when I was needed, otherwise at Umanak, between the two, as ordered by Mac. Hovey seemed to think that in doing so I was cut off from Etah if needed there. Nonsense. I cannot remember how many times I have made that trip.

Captain Pickles of the *Cluett* had sold for personal profit most of the emergency provisions he had contracted to carry, so we had to provision the ship as much as we could from Etah. That was a hard, hungry winter. Except for oatmeal and beans, the *Cluett* never had enough supplies, and Freuchen wasn't much better off at Umanak because the war had reduced supplies from Denmark, so, as always, whenever I could, I hunted. Dr. E.O. Hovey, Chairman of the Crocker Land Committee of the Museum, had come along on the ship, thinking, of course, to return the same summer. He was in no condition to withstand the rigors of Arctic existence and required my attention much of the time, although his health improved remarkably.

We had very little and late news of the war. The navy men wanted to go home, and Mac sent Tank, Allen, and Green sledging to South Greenland with Freuchen and the mail in January of 1916, to go home via Denmark, on a route I took in different circumstances the following winter.

ON BOARD *CLUETT*, PARKER SNOW BAY
Greenland, January 10, 1916

Dear Uncle Rich:

We are in a good deep bay, some 50 miles north of Cape York, on the Greenland coast, and about the same distance south of Umanak.

MacMillan and Small are at Etah. In a few days Green, Allen, Tanquary, and Dr. Hovey, the museum representative, start south with five or six Eskimo sledges to reach the Danish colonies and catch the first ship to Europe (if there is any such place now) in April.

The expedition has rented a house at Umanak for Ekblaw, Captain Comer, and me, and there is a partial store of food there. Supplies are already short here on the ship. Etah is somewhat better off. I am stationed between the ship and Etah in order to be an ever present help in time of trouble.

Things are at sixes or sevens due to poor judgment or, possibly, dishonesty. The *Cluett* is a well-built motor schooner, but has a poor engine, and that broke down finally. Also, as I have said, she has not enough food. I expect to see scurvy before spring among the crew, but am in no danger myself. Beans and salt horse are not good for a prolonged diet, and flour will be gone soon, if the Captain tells the truth.

War news up to last June is at hand. I believe the United States seeks peace at the price of dishonor. If one sees a man go into a neighbor's house and mistreat or murder the peaceful inhabitants, his duty is plain. A polite note of protest becomes in such a case ridiculous. Also our lax naval and army program is unsafe. Japan is not to be trusted.

Mac's attitude has discouraged scientific work, and little has been done. Unwise use of the food supplies has reduced them to unsafe limits, and there has been dishonest use of them in trading for fox skins. There is no bad feeling among us, but a desire to be quit of the expedition.

My news from Bangor is all good, and I hope Father will hold onto his money long enough to spend it on himself. He deserves it.

I have no plans on getting back, but should study at some postgraduate school immediately. After that I must provide a home and shall hope for more children. I am not eager to settle in a doctor-ridden city, but would like to be near Father and Mother. Barb [Hal's sister] is doing well and should succeed. I think she has a chance to do more than well if she is given her head.

In case Aunt Mary does not get well I hope you will consider my home (wherever it may be) as yours. Marion and I seek happiness only.

Affectionately,
Hal

Marion received not only letters from Hal and from the returning members of the expedition, but also the following from Hal's sister, Barbara Hunt, M.D.

WASHINGTON D.C.
Sunday evening, 1916

Dear Marion:

I suppose you have heard how I operated on Mrs. Jerome Allen for appendicitis last Monday. She is still in the hospital of course, and I am just returning to Baltimore after a trip over here to see her. She is doing fine and going home in a few days. She has had no setback, and the incision looks splendid: McBurney's incision. I could not get any skin clips, so sewed up with subcutaneous suture, which has left a very fine scar. She said the interns told her it was a fine operation! Between us, they ought to know, for their eyes stuck out a foot they were so curious to see how I did it!

Mrs. Allen is a dear bright young girl. Mr. Allen has told me a lot about Hal. I wish you could hear him talk. He makes it very clear and interesting. He said that Hal had missed you and Ruth bitterly, and he had heard him regret having come, before the first year was over.

He told me something else, which is to be kept very quiet, that last fall, when they thought Mac was behaving so badly, it was agreed by all the rest, even Green, that if the command had to be taken from Mac, it would be best to give it to Hal. This was before Hovey came. Hovey and Mac were jealous of each other before the expedition started. Did you know that? And they scrapped all the time up North. Allen says Hal's best friend is Peter Freuchen, whom he really enjoys.

Allen showed me a report of a trip he took, about 200 miles, to get moving pictures, down to North Star Bay, to Freuchen's trading station and out to an island where great quantities of duck nest. It was a summer trip, alternating snow and thaw, and with much traveling up and down the glaciers, trying to make stops at Eskimo settlements.

I asked Allen why they selected Hal for command of the expedition if necessary. He said they all felt he would be fair to everyone, he was the oldest, and also he was the one most accustomed to running a family. However, it didn't come to that, ever.

He thought there might be trouble when the expedition got back, between Mac and Hovey about skins Mac wanted to keep for himself or give to Bowdoin College. He said Mac had offered Hal a bear skin to give to Bowdoin, but Hal had refused it, saying that the furs did not belong to Mac to give away, that they belonged to the museum.

Have to stop now, love,
B-

I would have been glad to go home with Tank, Allen, and Green, and had hoped to do so, but I had orders from Mac to stay at Umanak. Dr. Hovey wanted to go along and also to be the leader. Allen and I told him he was not fit to lead. He did not know Arctic conditions. He insisted. He left with a dog team and an Eskimo guide to go south, ahead of the others. When he had gone about 50 miles, he sent back word that he had had a heart attack and asked for me to come down. He could not go on. I had started on a rush call 50 miles north, where an Eskimo was badly injured. He had been using a killing iron as a hitching post for his dogs. They had snapped it out of the ice, and it had driven deep into his thigh.

After I took care of him, I went to Hovey. He called the Eskimos savages and treated them with contempt. He once remarked to me that all that counted in life was money, anyway. I did not like to deal with him.

Captain Comer, the ice pilot of the *Cluett* and an old whaling captain, was fine. He was big physically and mentally. He stood over six feet tall and weighed over 200 pounds. He had a bronzed, round face with a moustache, frank blue eyes, and a kindly voice. We were good friends, and he was a good man in the Arctic, which the other men on the *Cluett* were not. I remember one day one of the men went hunting, and word was brought that he was frozen, about four miles away. I took a search party of three and went after him. When we got to him, he was unable to move, speak, or so much as open his mouth to drink the hot soup we had brought him. He was way up on a high bluff, and the only thing to do was to bring him down to the ship. Two of the men held him upright, and I got under him and took him piggyback, holding his hands about my neck, just as I used to carry Ruth. He would slump back and was hard to carry, as he was quite a heavy man and a dead weight. The going was all downhill. I carried him a mile and a half, and then we lowered him down the face of the cliff to where we had been obliged to leave the sledge. It was dark and very cold. I had brought a pair of boots for him, and took off my mittens and put them on him. We hauled him to the ship, stripped him on the table, and warmed him up. Even then, he could not speak, but we wrapped him up and kept him warm, and he came out all right except for a little frostbite on his toes.

I was glad when I could leave the *Cluett*, where there was much discord, to stay with Peter Freuchen and Navarana at Umanak, and they were glad to have me. Peter was extremely ill that summer of 1916. He maintained that I saved his life. I don't know about that, but I spent the better part of two months nursing him back to health.

It was then, at Umanak, which Knud and Peter had renamed Thule, that Captain Comer and I dug out the kitchen midden: the garbage and trash of hundreds, perhaps thousands of years of human habitation, and which later became known as Comer's midden in archeological studies. As we dug, it thawed about two inches a day. We found tools that even the Eskimos there could not identify. Later Rasmussen found the same type of artifacts in northern Canada, and named the culture that had produced them the Thule culture.

Ekblaw was with us a good part of that summer, too. There was one thing Ek wanted most of all, and that was to find the nest and eggs of the knot (*Tringa canutus*), which had never been found, although ornithologists had searched for it for many years, all over northern Asia and America. Many days Ek and I had hunted for it from Etah. We would take two sticks with a rope between them and go carefully over the ground to raise a bird, but we had no luck. One day at Thule I was out alone and all of a sudden nearly stepped on one. There the bird was, sitting on the nest with three eggs in it, just in a hollow in a grassy spot among the rocks. The bird and eggs, both the color of an old shingle mottled with brown, were almost invisible. I had to poke the bird to make her move off the nest. I marked the nest with a long line of stones and went for Ek. When we came back, we photographed the bird, nest, and eggs, and then, although we hated to do it, we shot the bird, carefully cut the nest out of the ground, and packed everything for the Museum. Later I came across another nest with four eggs in it. Both nests were on an upland a mile from the shore and not far from the icecap. The knot is about as big as a pigeon and flies as far south as Patagonia in the winter.

When the *Cluett* came free of the ice in July, she sailed with no passengers. Not even Captain Comer was happy to try the engineless old schooner, now dragging a damaged propeller. She did eventually get home safely, after much trouble with ice and heavy seas. We were all certain a new and abler ship would come for us that summer.

Summer can be a hungry time, too, and that was a hungry summer. Birds and eggs we had, but not much meat. We didn't even have dog biscuit at Umanak. Every fall the bears came south over the glacier to the head of Wolstenholm Sound, to go seal hunting as soon as the seals had to use blow holes through the ice to breathe. We were glad when they came, because one of those polar bears will feed a lot of people and dogs. I shot a big one while I was Knud's guest, and he gave me the skin for my wife. The bears used to come right down where the Thule Air Base is now, the only place where there is plenty of flat land for an airfield. It extends way back to the icecap.

On September 13, 1916, the old Danish vessel, *Danmark*, arrived at Umanak as our second relief ship, even later in the season than the *Cluett*, and was unable to proceed to Etah. The Museum had tried to save money by allowing her to pick up some freight, and so delayed her voyage north. Thus the *Danmark* got frozen in at North Star Bay over the winter of 1916-1917. Ek and I lived aboard until we left in December of 1916. We ate well: oatmeal, canned fruit, vegetables, and corned beef, blood pudding, walrus, and other fresh meats. But the *Danmark* was, Ek and I considered, short of coal, and never could make it to Etah and home under power. Why couldn't they send a properly equipped ship?

In October it must have been, some Eskimos arrived from Kangerdlookswa with news of an injury to my friend, Sigloo, of North Pole fame, so I got lots of gauze, etc., from Freuchen. Pastor Olsen, the Greenlander missionary at Umanak, Inyougeeto, and I sledged two long days on good ice to get there. We found a warm welcome, Sigloo comfortable, and his back injury well. However, his right foot was necrotic, the small ankle bones crushed, and the skin on the sole dead clear to the heel and very foul.

Inyougeeto gave chloroform, Pastor Olsen assisted me, and both did well. I removed the foot at the ankle joint. Sigloo did not suffer from shock and recovered rapidly. The skin flaps were scanty but remained firm and healed well. Early in November, we returned to the ship. We found deep snow on the glacier and had hard sledging.

The presence of Hovey, Chairman of the Crocker Land Committee of the Museum, made it difficult to know who was in charge. Hovey and Mac each thought *he* was. Hovey had given me permission to leave on the *Cluett*, which was in no condition to get to Etah to pick up the whole expedition. Ek, whom Mac had placed in charge of the substation at Umanak, also had urged me to go, and for a while I had been tempted to accept Hovey's or Ek's authority and to sail south, even in such an inadequately equipped and poorly manned sailing ship. How I wanted out, and how I longed for home! Poor Ek, I must have been hard to live with. It had taken me some time to accept the fact that I was, except in case of necessity, under an obligation to stay at Umanak according to my written orders from Mac. I had signed that contract that said Mac was the sole leader, and full obedience was to be accorded to his orders.

When I finally left Umanak I traveled under Mac's written instructions, and with Hovey's authorization also.

The Polar Inuit do their traveling in winter and early spring because one can sledge then on the ice foot and sea ice. With good weather one could not ask for better conditions than during the eight days each month that the winter moon is continuously above the horizon. Accordingly, Mac ordered Ek and me, at Umanak, to sledge south, starting with the December moon [1916], to catch the first ship from South Greenland for Denmark in the spring of 1917. We were eager to be off, to be shut of the whole expedition, although sad to say goodbye to our good Eskimo friends, whom we would probably never see again. We would go with the mail, as Tank, Green, and Allen had done the previous year.

X

Umanak to South Upernavik December 18, 1916 - February 14, 1917

THE OLD SCHOONER *Danmark's* supply of coal was so low she might have trouble getting out the next summer, so Mac had ordered Ek and me to sledge south down the coast about 1,300 miles to Holsteinsborg, South Greenland, there to catch the first Danish steamer to the Faroe Islands and Denmark, in order to notify the American Museum in New York that their second relief ship had failed. It was absolutely necessary for the rest of the expedition to be relieved the following summer with a sufficiently sturdy boat, and in good time to avoid being frozen in again over the winter. Knud Rasmussen was departing with mail and furs for Upernavik when the moon was full in December. He would take us along with him, and he was to be in charge. We should be in Tasiussak by Christmas, Upernavik by New Year's, and Holsteinsborg soon thereafter, traveling by dog sled on land-fast sea ice all the way, but weather conditions during the whole trip proved unusual.

We started south from Umanak the eighteenth of December, 1916, Knud, Ek, and I, with five Eskimos and their women, children, and dog teams, about 70 dogs. We traveled by moonlight and starlight. We did not leave until the tail end of the continuous moonlight, as mail from Etah had been delayed. The weather was rather stormy and very cold. The snow was too soft for snow houses, so we had arranged to sleep in tents, not an ideal arrangement. A tent is the coldest place in cold weather. Frost from one's breath forms inside and falls like snow over the sleepers. I had a caribou sleeping bag and two blankets, and was warm sleeping outside.

As planned, we covered 50 miles on each of the first two marches, bringing us to the Eskimo settlement at Cape York. For several days, we stayed there, divided among the five igloos and stuffed with Eskimo food:

seal, walrus, bear, and narwhal, especially the raw skin of the narwhal, a great Eskimo delicacy, tasting much like mushrooms. We now had about 90 miles as the crow flies to cross the sea ice of Melville Bay to Cape Seddon, the last of the Polar Inuit settlements. [The distance measures 140 miles on Operational Navigation Chart ONC B-8.] Normally, this is a trip of about three days, but at Cape York we found conditions not very good. Snow was falling. The snow was already soft and deep, six or eight inches, with slush underneath and a light crust on top, which the dogs broke through. *Pootenook* the Eskimos call it, the very worst traveling. The sledges sat down in the snow and were hard to pull.

I could see the expedition was poorly planned. Rasmussen had elected to take along five women with several children. The dogs were poor, and the sleds going south with us were heavily loaded: about twelve seals for dog food, sleeping bags, extra clothing, mail, and hundreds of fox skins for trading. Rasmussen paid no attention to the fact that the dogs were in poor shape, the traveling bad, and the sledges overloaded. When I looked things over, I made up my mind that I wanted a sled of my own to push on ahead if necessary. I spoke to Rasmussen, and he agreed. Then I spoke to Ooqueea, my Eskimo friend from Cape York, and asked him if he would go with me to Upernavik with his sledge. He was glad to go, and the next morning we started out on the ice across Melville Bay. Ooqueea had no baggage. I had only my sleeping bag, an extra pair of footgear, and my copy of Robert Browning, so we could travel light if we needed to go ahead of the others.

Ooqueea was a pippin. When I asked him to come with me, he did not hesitate, although he had no sleeping bag or equipment, only a piece of bearskin to sleep on, while I had the two blankets and the caribou bag. I tried to make him take one or the other, but he just lay down on his bearskin on the snow and went to sleep. I thought he would freeze, but he didn't even complain. He did eventually use my caribou *kooletah*, however, which helped him a lot, enough for him to sleep in comfort.

Ooqueea was the best bear hunter at Cape York. He was short, thin, and looked more like a Chinese mandarin than like the other Greenland Eskimos. He had thin whiskers on his chin. His right leg was useless from the knee down. I can see him now, as he tried to keep up with me across the soft snow. He hung onto the uprights of the sled, swung out his lame leg, and brought it toward the upright to hurry forward, plodding along that way all day behind the sled. He had been to the North Pole with Peary, who said: "Before he had paralysis he was the best man I ever had." He made no reference, ever, to his disability. When I asked him about it, he said that it just happened that way, that it was not due to an accident or sickness. It was almost typical of the results of anterior poliomyelitis. He knew some English but would not speak it. He always called me *Nanookswa*. He was like a blood brother to me. When I left, I loaded him with everything I could possibly do without. Once in a lifetime you see a man like that — modest, cheerful, not asking anything, but giving his all and meeting circumstances the best way he knows how. It would be difficult to better him.

The *pootenook* made slow going and was exceedingly hard on both dogs and men. I broke trail because I had snowshoes. The Eskimos were never interested in learning how to use them, and I could not understand this, as they were often valuable. Luckily, my snowshoes fitted my feet perfectly, and the harness was working well, so that I could walk all day steadily. Dogs will follow a track, even when hungry and tired, until they drop, but will wander and make a crooked trail if you try to drive them. The soft snow made it too difficult for them, with their small feet, to pull, and the sledges were too heavily loaded. So, to pack the snow down for the dogs with my snowshoes, I broke trail all the way.

This was, mind you, in the middle of winter, dark, no light from the sun. Rasmussen and I conferred and decided we would travel by the stars. By this time, the moon had mostly disappeared, and since at noon there was only a faint tinge of light from the south, the traveling was rather blind. We were constantly stumbling up against icebergs, or falling as we struck a piece of rough ice. You could not see an iceberg ten feet away, but you could see the stars. Every morning we decided which star to follow, and I shifted my course little by little to the left as the star moved around. We had no light or compass, not even a watch, but we could hear the sea on our right and knew the softer, deeper snow was on our left. The lack of a compass did not matter. We were so close to the magnetic pole that it would have been unreliable. In any case, we had no light to see a compass with. Traveling by the stars was better.

We did not dare to get out onto the sea ice too far, but neither did we want to get into the deep snow that lay along the coast to our left. Usually when sledging we followed the coast and could see the shore, but on this trip we could see only mist and soft snow.

I trudged ahead of the dogs steadily and had to go very slowly not to get too far ahead. When I did, Ooqueea came up to me and warned me not to, for bears would be around and hungry at that time of year. So I traveled slowly — we figured about one and a half miles an hour, twelve hours a day. My work snowshoeing ahead of the sledges did not let me see what was going on behind. One day I snowshoed 18 hours. Rasmussen sent ahead to tell me I must stop because the dogs were tired out, so I found a good iceberg, and we stopped.

We always camped at the end of a march in the lee of an iceberg, to obtain shelter from the wind and have fresh water from the berg ice to make tea and cook meat with. It took us perhaps two hours to get settled in our sleeping bags and about the same time to get away in the morning. We never ate at noon.

To make camp, first one found an iceberg with , in its lee, a firm surface and no slush. The dogs were unhitched from the sledges, fastened each team by itself, and fed. Next the sledges were pushed up ready to be placed on the flap of the tent to hold it down. The tent itself was unrolled, the poles inside erected, and the sides were pulled out and made fast underneath and to the sledges. Skins and sleeping bags were placed in order in the back part of the tent. Stoves and provisions were brought in, with a large lump chipped off the corner of the iceberg. For light, a candle or Eskimo *ikama* was lit. One person started the primus stove, another filled the kettle with cracked ice, and tea was ready in about 20 minutes. In the meantime, if there were any meat around, everyone would be chipping off pieces of frozen meat with a knife and eating it raw.

Sometimes we were too weary to cook any food but made our meal of tea, frozen, raw meat, and ship biscuits (hardtack). Our sleeping equipment was excellent, which was just as well, as the weather was about 50 or 60 degrees below zero for 10 days. Knud said he had never seen it so cold on Melville Bay.

That Christmas Eve I shall never forget. The going was terrible. A bitter wind blew down from the icecap, and a damp fog came up. I could see only a star above me, nothing around me. I got snowshoe lameness. Ek froze both big toes. He pluckily continued to walk, however, until we both decided it was safer for him to protect his feet from further injury by riding. Luckily, I escaped like misfortune. For a long time I could not find an iceberg where we could pitch our tent. When I did, we were wet with sweat. We shivered when we stopped traveling as though we would never get warm. Ooqueea had found some bear meat he had cached in November, so we ate bear meat and drank tea. For our Christmas dinner Ek brought out some dates he had saved, and Knud produced some canned pears. In our sleeping bags we sang "Silent Night" in English and Danish while the Eskimos hummed the tune.

One day was like another, and we traveled nine days. It was after the third day that food started to run short, so we were all, dogs and men, on half rations, and we were working hard. Our supper was one pannikin of tea and a sandwich of two ship biscuits with a slice of bear meat or bear fat. The dogs became weaker and more difficult to urge forward. They began to gnaw at their sealskin traces. Three died, and we fed what was left of them to the others. After a week, no one could tell where we were, and Rasmussen decided he should take a few of the best dogs, and with no load, go ahead to see if he could find the Eskimo village at Cape Seddon to get a rescue team. I wasn't worried and crawled into my sleeping bag and went to sleep. I was dog-tired and hungry, but I can sleep anytime. I had led the way for a week; I was strong then and loved to use my strength. I could lift a loaded sled and help the dogs up the side of a cliff, a sled that the little Eskimos could not budge.

Next thing I knew, Ek was shaking me. "Hal," he said, "We had better be going somewhere. Knud has not come back, and I am worried. The dogs are dying."

"Oh," I said, "Don't worry," and I turned over to sleep again.

"Hal," said Ek, "You have been sleeping for two days, and we have no food left. We must go on. I think the other team is lost." So we moved forward. The visibility had improved somewhat. We climbed the first big iceberg, and there at noon we could see the silhouette of a coastline to the north.

"I know where we are," Ooqueea said, "I lived in that country one or two seasons. We'll be at the settlement within an hour." We had been headed in the right direction all the time, though Rasmussen had gone off the wrong way when he left us.

We stacked all unessentials to lighten the sledges for the weary dogs and headed for shore. I led the way; otherwise the dogs would not move. I would take off one snowshoe to ease the pain in the tendon that gets so lame lifting a snowshoe, and then I would put that one on and take off the other, but the pain would come back just the same. Ever tried walking with one snowshoe off and one on? If I took both off, the dogs could not follow in the deep snow. After seven hours, the shore seemed just as far away as ever in the misty whiteness, but finally we were seen, and a rescue team came out to meet us. Rasmussen had just arrived, too. More dogs had died on the way. We were fortunate to make it the day we did.

I headed for the nearest hut and called down the hole at the top: "Call off the dogs!" I dropped on all fours, crawled inside, never asking if I could, pushed over the sleeping figures, and without a word, snuggled down to sleep in the extreme left-hand corner.

When I awoke, four Eskimos were pulling hard on a sealskin line, jerking half a frozen narwhal through the tunnel. They stood it up on end at the entrance to the igloo — it was a very large igloo. We all went at it with a hatchet and hacked off frozen pieces to eat raw. It tasted wonderful to me. The best food I ever ate, and it did not disagree with anyone. Our ship biscuits, sugar, and coffee were, however, gone. I went to sleep again.

Ek woke me up, saying, "Hal, I've got a bad nosebleed."

I said, "Well, that's all right. They always stop."

"This one hasn't," he said, "and I've bled a whole tomato canful of blood." I got out my bag, plugged both nostrils, and stopped the bleeding. He thought he had frosted the inside of his nostrils. I don't think so; it was probably high blood pressure and overexertion.

Next day, an Eskimo asked me to see a sick woman. I found her in severe pain with a bad case of shingles running around from her spine at the waistline in big, bad blisters. I could relieve the pain somewhat but had nothing to control the intense itching. At least I could tell them she would not die, and would even soon be well.

The Eskimos at Cape Seddon were very good to us; everything they had was ours. People who have little always share; they know what it is to be without. For three days we rested the dogs, dried out our sleeping bags and clothing, and then, with three extra teams, began the next stage to Tasiussak, the first Danish trading station. To avoid the deep snow, we went offshore onto the new, thin ice. This brought us into rough, broken-up ice fields, which was tough on the sledges. Two had to be mended that night. The following day, as we were planning to camp, we met two South Greenland Eskimos with dog teams who had been bear hunting and had secured one small bear. In the midst of a sudden heavy snowstorm, we made camp with the two strangers, sharing our tea with them and getting bear meat in return. From this point on, Eskimo villages were common, and the Eskimos had a well-worn path along the shore. In many places we saw that the Eskimos had seal nets under the ice, a new thing to us, as the Polar Inuit do not use nets.

On January 6, 1917, we arrived at Tasiussak, where Mr. Neilson and his Eskimo wife entertained us for two days. Like almost every village where I stopped from there on, Tasiussak was on one of the myriad islands studding this part of the Greenland coast. We saw no more cold weather until the end of March, but instead, for the next two and a half months, the warmest weather the Eskimos could remember for this time of year, and from then on, everywhere, meat was scarce due to the bad hunting weather. We heard the ice was rotten, and heavy wind had recently broken it up between Tasiussak and Upernavik. We left our worn-out dogs for Rasmussen to take back to Cape York with him later and engaged six teams for the two-day trip to Upernavik, even though the South Greenland dog teams were not as good as those of the Polar Inuit. They lacked both size and training.

The South Greenland Inuit themselves were not as hardy and independent as the Polar Inuit. They seemed poverty stricken, and the houses were too hot and poorly ventilated. Cloth spreads had taken the place of skins on the bed platforms, and they were dirty and uninviting. From then on, we found tuberculosis prevalent every place we stopped. Eskimos were continually coming to me for medical treatment.

Sometimes we were forced to go overland for short distances, but it was now light enough to see at noon. Mostly the sledging was good, and the dogs romped along at about seven miles an hour. We reached Upernavik the evening of the second day. There, we saw the first wooden houses since Umanak. Ekblaw stayed with the Governor, Rasmussen with the nurse, and I with the doctor, who did not play chess, but who drank good, black Danish coffee with me six times a day.

Leaving Upernavik, we were forced by stretches of thin ice and open water to make a detour to Augtapalartok, at right angles to our course. Two more days' sledging took us to Proven. There, Rasmussen and his crowd started back to Cape York, having left their trading goods. There I had to say goodbye to Ooqueea, he to return home. He was a fine man indeed, and I would trust him in any emergency. I told him so and gave him all the presents he could possibly take back with him. He had looked after me as though I were a baby.

With our new outfit, Ek and I easily crossed the bay to South Upernavik, a very comfortable place. The ice to the south was bad, and we waited two weeks for ice to form in the fiord. The Eskimos danced in an old schoolhouse and never got tired, although the accordion player had to be relieved from time to time. I supplied them with tobacco, which made them very happy, as they had not been able to get to the trading post for many months.

When ice did form, they went out frequently to test it. An Eskimo is used to traveling on thin ice; he does it all his life. He uses a chisel stick sometimes to test the thickness ahead, or just crawls out on all fours to feel the bend. He knows how much it will stand. Finally, although the ice was very thin indeed, they announced they would go. We let the dogs out 40 feet ahead of the sledge, as the ice would bend under them, and this kept a wave of ice between the dogs and the sledge. Thus, if a dog went through, the sledge could be saved.

South Upernavik is on the outer end of a long island that forms the northern side of a fiord. We crossed the fiord and for two days tried to get around the headland of the peninsula forming its southern side. Open water turned us back. On the second night a big blizzard came. It ripped our tent off us and sent it scurrying up the bay. I was in my sleeping bag, and it is difficult to get out of a bag and into clothes in a driving, snow-laden wind, but I got out and caught up with the badly torn tent sailing along on the ice in heavy wind and snow. On the next day we pushed up the bay on the edge of an open lead and found we could not get around that way either. With some trouble we returned to South Upernavik.

Ek and I talked about the possibility of going on, of getting to Holsteinsborg in time for the boat. Ek didn't believe it could be done, given the many delays and the open season. I figured I could, somehow. Since there were not many good dogs available, we both agreed that one man might make it more likely than two, and that I should go ahead alone.

It was important to get our message through. I was in excellent physical condition, but the extreme hardship of the Melville Bay crossing had taken its toll of Ek's physique, and his feet were still sore. I hated to leave him, as he had been the best of companions in all circumstances. He would go back to Upernavik and in the summer take a Danish boat to Godhavn, where a relief ship would eventually pick him up.

I was determined to get out and willing to make any personal sacrifice in an attempt to do so.

XI

South Upernavik to Agto February 15-March 21, 1917

ACROSS THE FIORD from South Upernavik, the shore of the peninsula is a long, very steep bluff. No one, the Eskimos said, had ever climbed it or gone into the mountains beyond. Since our way was barred around the bluff, we *had* to climb it and go through the mountains. It was difficult to get men and dogs to go on a route never tried before, but I always was obstinate. On February fifteenth, paying double wages, I started out with three sledges, two local men, and Tobias, an Eskimo whom Rasmussen had hired to accompany me. The whole village turned out with all available dogs and sealskin lines to haul us up the bluff.

After seeing me up the hill, Ekblaw and the others turned back. Although my three Eskimos had never gone overland there before, and the dogs were in rather poor shape from the day's hard pull, we camped comfortably that night, in a tent. After we had gone behind the headland, we came down a valley through soft snow to sea ice and familiar territory again.

This part of the coast of Greenland is a maze of islands and deep fiords. The headlands are black, precipitous cliffs. There is no flat land, only mountains. Glaciers from the icecap discharge into the heads of the fiords, where ice is apt to remain frozen until summer, whereas strong tides at the mouth keep the water open, swirling around icebergs and ice floes, sweeping them pell-mell out to sea.

I sledged overland and across thin ice from village to village, changing guides with their dog teams at each village wherever possible, as generally the Eskimos were knowledgeable about the territory only within, say, 50 miles of home. Again, in many places, I went where even the local Eskimos had never been before. Few white men, if any, had ever been to these villages, and I think, no Americans. The Eskimos' eyes nearly popped out of their heads when I appeared, often from a direction they thought impossible. When I told them who I was, and how I must hurry, and showed them a picture of my wife and little girl, they said to each other, "Poor man, he wants to get home. He is homesick," and they did their best for me.

I felt keenly the lack of a map. The normal highway along the coast on the land-fast sea ice was unusable, an unheard-of condition for the middle of the winter, yet there was too much ice to use a boat. Once, we found a place where we could not in any way go forward. We went up the fiord to get around, but found an open lead. I told my Eskimo guides to go back home, and I would wait until it froze solid, but they said they would stay with *Nagorsakswa*. I traveled light: just a tent, bag, extra footgear, the mail, and a little food. Now I was out of food and had no trading goods or tobacco, but they stayed right with me. We waited two days and finally crept hesitantly over newly formed swaying ice to the land. There, we fastened the dog teams and walked across the mouth of a fiord on ice too thin for sledges, to get to the village that night. Next morning, it was all blue water where we had crossed. We went back overland, around the head of the fiord, to get the dogs and bring them to the village.

We had to cross the wide peninsula of Svartenhuk. I led the way uphill all day on snowshoes through about 10 inches of loose snow. The Eskimos were using skis, the first time I had seen them do that. We were loaded with five seals, sugar, coffee, tobacco, kerosene, guns, sleeping bags, and one tent. The Eskimos there do not know how to make snow houses, since the snow is rarely of the right consistency. We stopped in a valley and fed the dogs well but were too tired to get anything more than tea and crackers for ourselves. One difficulty in land travel is to find ice to melt for drinking water and cooking. On the sea, there usually are plenty of freshwater floes and icebergs. After working and sweating all day, we suffered an agonizing thirst waiting to drink, as each potful of snow melting over our stove produced water only by the spoonful. We promised ourselves a feast in the morning, so the next morning we had seal meat, ship biscuits, and sugar in our coffee. It was snowing briskly, and all landmarks were indistinct, but the Eskimos were willing to move, and we got an early start. We had an unexplored route ahead of us, with the possibility of delay and shortage of food. We had to make headway at every opportunity. I started off ahead of the sledges, plodding along, keeping out of the deepest snow in the bottom of the valley, staying up on the slopes, where the snow was partly blown away. The tops of the hills were rough, bare rock.

We now had four or five hours of sunshine a day, and the weather cleared about noon. The Eskimos pointed out to me the mountains at the far shore of the peninsula, so I headed for them down a natural pass winding through the hills. The snow became deeper, and the teams fell far behind, because the heavy snow had made the dogs footsore. Balls of snow formed in the hair between the dogs' toes and had to be cut out. Sometimes the Eskimos use little boots on the dogs to prevent this, but we had none. At dusk I packed down a place to pitch the tent. Although we had not seen the sea to know where we were, we felt certain we were nearing sea level and would find our way through the hills the next day. The loads were getting lighter each day, and our meat was running low, but the Eskimos assured me we could kill seal as soon as we came to the next fiord, Umiavik, meaning a bay where one can go with a skin boat.

Sure enough, next morning after about three hours' sledging we reached sea ice. Seals were up on the ice in several places, but in two attempts the Eskimos failed to get one. The snow was still heavy and still necessitated a trail breaker ahead. My snowshoe lameness was starting up again. We were going across the mouth of a deep inlet about six miles broad when, nearing the opposite shore about dusk, we shot a small seal, so we made camp on the ice foot near by, cut up the seal, fed part to the dogs, and ate the rest.

Next morning about daylight, the tent blew away, ripped from end to end. We had to chase and repair it. The weather was very warm; there was water on the ice all day, which made it easier for the dogs, and we were able to ride almost all day. We were headed off by open water again and had to make a detour inland behind some islands to country unknown to these Eskimos. Late in the afternoon we saw a strange Eskimo hunting seal, and through him we reached the settlement of Nuliavik. I paid the Eskimos 68 kroner each: 30 Danish miles at two kroner a mile, and the rest for the dogs. A Danish mile is equal to four of ours, and a kroner was 26 cents. This was double the regular wages but the men had earned it all right.

We were all put up in the schoolhouse, built of sod and rocks, roofed and floored with boards, a commodious shelter, although there was no method of heating it. We boiled meat and made tea on our primus stove, and all the Eskimos of the village crowded around. Our ship biscuits and sugar were gone, and we were living exclusively on seal meat. The igloos were crowded and very dirty, the schoolhouse cold and uncomfortable, and food scarce. There was no store, and we expected none at the next village either.

Nuliavik lay on the extreme end of a long island, and there was open water on three sides when we arrived. We could not continue by sledge. I sent a kayak on to the next settlement to report on the ice beyond, hoping to transfer the sledges to solid ice by *umiak*. That night the wind took out the remaining ice, although it was cold and snowing. We could only hope for better weather for either sledging or boating. The second day the kayak man came back, reporting poor ice, but new ice had started to form, and we hoped it would be solid in a couple of days.

There were some dogs to be had, and since Rasmussen had promised that we would give Tobias a team, I advanced him money to buy them. Dr. Hovey had arranged with Rasmussen to take charge of the South Greenland trip as far as he could, and this was one of the results. Tobias had not had a team since Tasiussak, and he had been nothing but a continual expense and drag upon us.

I had to wait five days, buying seal meat to live on and losing strength as I always did when living solely on the Eskimo diet. I picked up two fine Eskimos at Nuliavik who were happy to go with me all the way to Jakobshavn: Peter the Bishop and Little Jonah. Peter was the village preacher and boss. He settled all quarrels in the village. He decided when to cross the ice. Jonah was bowlegged and tiny, looked like a little spider. He must have weighed about 80 pounds and always wanted to go first onto thin ice. He was renowned as the best hunter in South Greenland. If Peter and Jonah had a cigar, they thought they were kings.

Finally the ice became fairly strong to the south, and we started. After about 15 miles we were stopped by thin ice. Tobias shot a seal, and we had it for supper. I had just one gallon of kerosene left, so I cooked on a very smoky *ikama,* using blubber from Tobias's seal for fuel and a piece of my shirt for a wick. Next morning we started before daylight in a blizzard. We sledged up the fiord on the ice foot, then overland and across a stream and a glacier to the next fiord. About halfway down that fiord we ran into a big lead of open water with a glacier wall cutting us off on the other side.

We were near a village on the mainland where there was a store, but we could not get there. While we waited for ice to form, I found a lot of brushwood for a fire and the men hunted seals for the dogs and ourselves. For me, they saved the best of the seal, the frozen eyeballs. My stomach refused. We tried hard to get over the glacier but could not. Peter and Jonah stayed by me well, although the ice was very dangerous, and food and fuel scanty. Both were extremely good on thin ice and cheerful in the face of difficulties. They asked for a bonus, and I was glad to give it to them.

The weather was very fickle, one day warm, the next cold and windy. When the wind died down, ice began to form. After a couple of days (and Tobias told me I was two days behind the calendar), the ice looked strong to me.

I asked Peter if we couldn't go on as I was anxious to get south to catch the first mailboat out.

He said he would try it and crawled out on all fours. The ice held him, so we started. Soon the runners were cutting through, and we had to turn back hastily. We waited three days more — lucky, I guess, to get back to wait. Then Peter said we should try it again. I had a handful of rice in my pocket. You get thinner and thinner and weaker and weaker traveling on seal meat and tea alone. I cooked the rice over a little fire made with moss. We four ate it with our fingers and started over very thin ice, often skirting pools of water, the ice bending dangerously under the dogs and sleds. We were headed by many open leads but could see the small cluster of huts at the head of the bay.

As we walked along the edge of a wide lead toward them, I heard a loud shout behind me. Looking back, I saw Tobias, sledge, and dogs floundering in water. I had provided a long coil of sealskin line for each sled to carry, and had two local Eskimos instead of one guide only for just such an emergency. If one got in trouble, the others could help. If all went through, no rope was any good. I threw my coil out onto the ice. It slid toward Tobias slowly, like a live snake. He reached out, caught it, and tied it to his sledge. Peter, Jonah, and I hauled and, with difficulty, pulled him ashore, dogs, sled, and all. We stripped him naked at once. He was pretty numb by that time. We pulled clothing out of our bags that covered him somewhat, and taking him by the arms, we ran him up and down the shore hard and fast.

When we got near the settlement, we were forced to go overland on bare, very rocky ground, which wore out the sled runners and our tempers, broke the sledges, and exhausted the dogs. Once there, we found a small store with a native storekeeper. I bought coffee, sugar, ship biscuits, tobacco, *halle fiske* (halibut), and three seals, one for each team. The next morning, all that bay was rippling water. Ice was making, however, and we hoped to get to Ikerasak the following day.

Because of open water in that part of Greenland, we figured that for six days we had been making only about 18 miles a day, and those not all in the direction we wanted, far from it. It was slow progress, so we started out at daylight and traveled fast all day. The young ice was treacherous; we had to make detours and go over very rough land, finally lowering sledges and dogs down a cliff to the ice on our sealskin lines. We arrived at the island village of Ikerasak at eight in the evening, very tired. There Mr. Fleisher told me Tobias had been right, that I had lost two days somewhere. This was March fourth, and I had thought it was the second.

Since the mail had not been able to get through either way between Upernavik and points south, and I was determined to do so, I had become a mailman. We could not get out to the island community of Umanak [this is Umanak on Umanak Fiord, South Greenland, not Umanak, North Star Bay], where I was supposed to deliver some letters, so the next morning we left early to cross Nugsuak Peninsula to Qeqertaq. We found deep, drifting snow and a heavy head wind. I was on snowshoes all day. We arrived at Qeqertaq about nine in the evening, our clothes full of snow and the dogs all played out; Tobias had to leave one behind. It was a long, hard, stormy day.

Tobias went home from Qeqertaq, paid in full. He had the only primus stove, but I was able to buy one from an Eskimo because he had no oil. There was a good map, but I could not get it to take with me. The storekeepers there and at Ikerasak were Rasmussen's uncles on his mother's side. Rain and wind held us up for two days, so I had some lighter weight skin clothing made: a pair of watertight *kamiks*, two *anoraks*, or parkas, and a waterproof sleeping-bag cover.

Open water prevented taking the usual direct route to Ritenbenk, on the outside of a large island, so on the third day we left at six in the morning for Ator, on the inside of the island. After many detours around leads and thin ice, we arrived there at four p.m. The local drivers demanded more pay than was right to guide us across the island to Ritenbenk, so I decided to spend the night at Ator, leave the mail there for Ritenbenk, and head directly for Jakobshavn the next day.

On the way to Jakobshavn, open water forced us to go overland a long way around the heads of the fiords. The Eskimos pushed and I pulled sledges and dogs up over the hills, among rocks, and through heavy, wet snowdrifts. We had very hard work and broke a sledge. To find better snow for sledging, we finally went right up to the edge of the icecap. The weather was fine but too warm. When we got back to the shore, we met a man and his son who had been seal hunting, and who agreed to take me ahead so Peter and Jonah could go home. With less resolute men than these, I could not have made this trip, but the new man and his son were the most capable travelers I met in South Greenland. We went at a dogtrot all day long. Gosh, I sweated that day. I was strong in those days, but that father and son, light-weights, could outrun me. We ran, literally ran, all afternoon.

When we approached the village of Jakobshavn, they asked me where I wanted to go. I told them to the house of the Governor. This was about midnight of March eighth. They took me to a house that was all lighted up. I walked upstairs to where the lights were and lay down on a European couch, a real couch, and waited for someone to come. Soon two beautiful Danish girls in European dress came in. I had seen no white girls for four years, and no white man, nor anyone who could speak English since I had left Ek almost a month ago. I explained who I was, and they said, "We have just finished a banquet, and the food is still on the table, so please come and eat and have some coffee with us." I said I was not in good shape to come to a banquet, but they insisted, and I'm afraid I gobbled up all that was left. I must have smelled very bad. When you wear fur clothes and work and never wash them, they just stink, plain stink. I was dirty, sweaty, tired, hungry, and lousy. They made nothing of that whatever. They were extremely gracious young ladies.

A man came in who proved to be Governor Anderson. He took me to a room where there was a wooden tub of steaming water, soap, towels, and a feather bed with a feather puff. I can see those four clean walls and the warm steaming water and the white towels, I can see it now.

He said, "Now, Dr. Hunt, just take off your clothes and throw them outside. We can talk tomorrow. I know you are tired." So I took a nice bath and got into bed, feathers under me, feathers over me. The next morning my clothes were ready. They had apparently been washed in gasoline during the night.

The Governor invited me to go caribou hunting with him, but I told him I was sorry, I was in too much of a hurry to get south. I played chess with him all day, hired new Eskimos to go with me, and the following day left for Egedesminde via Christianshaab and Ikamiuk, which took us three long days. There, too, there was no sea ice at all, the worst year for hunting and travel the people had ever known. Wherever possible, we sledged on the ice foot; mostly we were forced to go overland on a very roundabout course, often hauling up or letting down the dogs and sleds on long lines over the cliffs.

At Egedesminde the weather kept me on the island for a week. It was exasperating to have bad weather so constantly, but I was very comfortable and was kindly cared for by Governor and Mrs. Fenker and Pastor and Mrs. Bolle. Mrs. Fenker mended and gave to me a pair of her husband's under-drawers, as the stores did not carry such things. I paid two kroner per day, room and board, and two or three kroner to each servant. The credit I had received from Rasmussen to cover the trip south ran out then, and I had to obtain money on my own credit. I got only enough to take me to Holsteinsborg, as I was certain credit from the Museum for any member of the expedition would arrive on the *Hans Egede*. Finally the weather turned cold, and when Pastor Bolle returned from a trip south he reported that I should try to go the following morning. He invited me to dinner and chess the last night, and afterwards we walked about four miles to see a sick Eskimo.

I went on to Agto by sledge, *umiak*, and kayak:

Field Notes:
March 18, 1917

Left Egedesminde for Neekornasuk with two sledges. Reached Kanasiak in the evening. For some reason the men took me here. Ice and snow good but the dogs poor.

March 19, 1917

Left at six a.m. for Neekornasuk and Iginiavik. The dogs are very poor and the men charge too much, but I can see nothing to do except pay the price. Took *umiak* across the fiord from Neekornasuk and from there sledged to Iginiavik. Warm and the snow is melting. Ice is covered with slush. Reached Iginiavik at eight in the evening. Very tired. Stayed with Mr. Johnsen, the Danish trader, who has only a very little English. Learn here that the snow and ice are bad for land travel to Holsteinsborg. It has snowed recently, and the warm weather here has spoiled the ice. I shall go to Ikerasarsuk tomorrow and try to get to Agto by boat.

March 20, 1917

Shall stay here at Iginiavik today and go on tomorrow if the weather permits. In the rain yesterday I got wet. Impossible to get to Holsteinsborg by sledge. Shall try to get to Agto and from there by boat. Rather trying to have bad weather. As the dogs deteriorate, the prices go up. They told me yesterday that last year the Americans paid 80 kroner where I paid for the same work 52 kroner. I had some trouble over prices but stuck to my own price and carried the day. Have sent a sled on today to see about the ice at Ikerasarsuk. He reports best to take the *umiak* from here to Agto, which I shall try to do. Am not well today. The wet, warm weather of yesterday with the long hours and heavy exertion of plunging through deep, soft snow has tired me very much. My clothes were wet to the skin from both sweat and rain. I feel confident, however, that I shall get through somehow.

March 21, 1917

Left Iginiavik at seven with two poor dog teams. Reached Ikerasarsuk at twelve. Took *umiak* and one kayak to the island settlement of Agto. The wind was onshore and made some waves and white caps, but the *umiak* behaved splendidly although the oars iced up some. There was much drift ice, but by going outside the islands we finally got to land about one mile from Agto and walked the rest of the way. The Eskimos were a good lot.[1]

[1]*Crocker Land Expedition Field Notes, No. 65, H.J. Hunt.* In Rare Books and Manuscripts Room of the American Museum of Natural History, New York.

XII

Agto to Holsteinsborg by Kayak March 21-April 22, 1917

IT WAS ON MARCH 21 that the Eskimo boatmen I had hired at Ikerasarsuk and I arrived at the little village on the small island of Agto — eight Eskimo huts a hundred miles north of Holsteinsborg.

There I was held three weary weeks by constantly changing weather. Two or three days of unseasonably cold weather would follow two or three of warm, southerly winds, neither holding long enough to make either sledging or boating possible. We had the motorboat in clear water once, only to have to run for the harbor before drifting floes bore down on us, which would have frozen us in out at sea. Inland lay 80 miles as the crow flies of unexplored land between us and the best of all roads, the Greenland icecap. Along the coast were bays and deep fiords of open water with furious tides pushing back and forth. On the sea, field upon field of pack ice jammed onto the coast, surging to and fro with the daily changes of wind or tide.

The one Dane at Agto, Hansen, was hospitality itself. In the little government store, where he traded with the Eskimos, during our meals, and over the nightly games of checkers, we discussed ways and means of getting the mail and myself the hundred miles to Holsteinsborg in time to catch the steamer. This was the last stage of the journey, and it had to be a success.

I thought of the inscription on the New York Post Office: "Neither snow, nor rain, nor heat, nor gloom of night stays these couriers from the swift completion of their appointed rounds," and I fretted.

Both Eskimo and Danish food was running low. The Eskimos could get nothing but a few cod each day, and Hansen had opened his last box of sugar until the boat came from Denmark.

At last the natives announced that from a point 15 miles south of Agto, on the outer side of an island, the tides were sufficiently active so that sea ice would no longer form. With good luck we might just be able to slip down between the pack and the shore in Eskimo skin boats, lifting out and carrying the boats over the barrier when jammed by ice, and watching our chance as tide and wind opened leads of water.

For the mail, we needed a so-called women's boat, an *umiak*. The *umiak* of the South Greenlander is a strongly built frame structure about 30 feet long, over which is laced a covering of skins of the Greenland seal, sewn together with sinew, so as to be watertight. These boats have a large carrying capacity, with the additional advantage that the crew of seven can lift it from the water and carry it for distances easily. By custom, a kayak man goes with such a boat as a sort of pilot, and I had a kayak built for myself while waiting. I realized there was some hard work ahead of us, and possibly the crew of the *umiak* might back out and not go at all. I was going through in any event, even if alone. I would not be deterred.

Hansen, who was to go south with the mail, enlisted all available dog teams, about 50 dogs, for the land part of the trip, and on the eighteenth of April we started. The *umiak* occupied one sledge, lying crosswise and being steadied by the crew. Two sledges were taken up by two kayaks, and the mail, food, tents, oars, and other supplies made the other four loads. Hansen, the Eskimos, and I walked. Snow had fallen recently, which made the 15 miles slow and difficult traveling. The first sledges got to the shore sometime after dark, the last, the one with the food, not until noon the next day. I was with the first and turned in dinnerless and supperless as well. It was very cold weather for that time of the year, and fortunately my sleeping bag had arrived on the first load.

The next morning showed a fringe of jumbled pack ice, about a quarter of a mile wide, fast to the shore, and beyond that a hurrying stream of ice fields as far as could be seen. Certainly by choosing tides we could make some progress. The weather was continually cold, about zero, with a sharp north wind ruffling the open leads. By one p.m. all the sledges were in from Agto; we had finished eating and were carrying boats and packages out over the rough fringe of solid floe ice to open water. The tide was full and would soon begin to ebb, bearing us south.

These South Greenland Eskimos are much more efficient boatmen than sledge men, in marked contrast to the Polar Eskimos, who are wonderfully able sledge men but not much accustomed to boating. I had some misgivings about my ability to follow the crowd in a kayak, and I noticed my companions watching me covertly as I pulled on my sealskin garments, both wind- and waterproof. The trousers tie at the waist and the ankles, and the coat at the wrists and the chin. A drawstring fastens the skirt of the coat tightly about the rim of the cockpit, making a practically watertight joint.

Soon all were afloat and hurrying south along the ice edge with a strong tide and wind to help. Ice blocked our way frequently, and dangerous loose ice, moving with wind and tide, was all about us. It was rough enough so that water slopped over my kayak, giving it a coating of ice, which soon increased to a deck load, with icicles hanging from the bow and stern. The paddle iced up badly. On the whole, however, I felt master of my craft, could keep up with the larger boat with its six oarsmen, and was warm and comfortable. To one accustomed to it, the South Greenland kayak is a perfect boat — light, swift, watertight, and warm. One learns to keep it right-side up by habit, but it can be righted if capsized, and that merely by the use of the paddle, while the low freeboard minimizes the force of wind or wave. Indeed it seems to be more at home in rough water than in smooth. There is none of the awkwardness of a canoe in a seaway, rather the smooth dip and rise of a well-found fishing smack.

Shortly before dusk we arrived at Arpek, which consisted of a group of deserted sod houses. Finding they were habitable, we decided to stay for the night. Boats were lifted out, stowed, and lashed. The houses were broken into by prying the sod coverings from the windows; two primus stoves were soon merrily buzzing, tea and meat boiled, and we were almost immediately asleep. Most of the natives had slept but little the night before and declared they could do much better work the next day if allowed a good rest now.

This proved to be so. They were really good men on the water.

Before daybreak we had a breakfast of strong coffee, and lots of it, with ship biscuit. After a careful survey of ice conditions, we were under way again. Continued cold weather with a slackening wind during the night had skimmed the open water with a coating of ice through which we pushed for several hours, only to have to retrace our path to land again. It was dreary, watching and waiting for a chance to go on. Finally, about noon, tide and wind combined to open a lead. A scarcely perceptible crack in a mile-square ice field gradually opened. Instantly we were making for that lead, backs bending and oars and paddles flashing. My companion kayak man was a fine young fellow, expert in his craft, but I thought my paddling muscles equal to his, and away we dashed, gaining slowly and finally overtaking the larger boat, when our way was barred by a bridge of ice, through which the *umiak* broke with undiminished speed.

Ahead lay open water, as far as the eye could see; to the left, a bold and broken coast line; out to sea, a mile distant, the drifting ice pack. At a steady pace of about five miles an hour, our little flotilla swept down the coast, a kayak on each side of the *umiak*, and ripples of foam about the bow of each. Eider ducks swarmed about us. We shot several without changing course. I was fortunate in getting a small, bearded seal, which lay sleeping on an ice cake, the meat of which we took for supper. Occasionally, loose ice, gathered in some tidal eddy, would bother us. Several times we landed to look ahead from the nearby hilltops, but there was no stop for dinner. A hasty mouthful of frozen, raw meat shared with me by the Eskimos seemed ambrosia.

About ten p.m. we camped on the north shore of Stromfiord, which winds inland about a hundred miles, right to the edge of the icecap. This is a place of unusually strong tides and was really the bar to our making the trip by dog sledge. The usual crossing places were open water this year, and no sledges had been able to make the trip during the whole winter. Hurrying masses of ice were now passing inland on the flood tide with frightful velocity. A bitter wind poured down the little hollow where we landed. It was midnight before we found a place with enough loose rocks to pitch the tents. Where pegs cannot be used, tent flaps must be pinned down by rocks.

Finally, the two tents were up, ice melted, tea made, and meat boiled, for at night we craved hot food. Low temperature and severe hardship increased the desire for meat to an intensity little dreamed of by the inexperienced, and as we set up the tents we snacked on frozen tidbits, which we were continually slicing off the seal with a knife. I am sure raw, frozen seal meat is much sweeter, and indeed more healthy than cooked. Convention and habit, in civilization, demand that it shall be cooked, and for sanitary purposes it may be necessary, but to the Eskimo, raw meat is a necessity without which he cannot exist.

The next morning we thought to cross the fiord on the high-tide slack, but when we were in the middle of the fiord, a very severe current came rushing out. It was extremely rough, so rough that they took me and the other kayak man aboard the *umiak*. We finally worked our way safely to the other side, where we could get back into the kayaks. There was considerable hazardous moving ice, and a bad wind behind us. Indeed, I was soon covered with ice from the water that constantly washed over my low kayak and dashed against me. Several times that day the accumulated ice had to be beaten from the skin boats. This is done with blunt-edged ice beaters made of caribou antler and commonly carried on all kayaks, slipped under one of the deck straps. The *umiak* made splendid weather of it and drifted like a feather before the wind owing to its high freeboard, while the kayaks, balancing on the crest of a wave, would shoot forward at express speed and suddenly drop into the trough. The double-bladed paddle had literally to be used as a balancing pole. There are few things in life more enjoyable than a day of such work.

Once we nearly came to grief. In attempting to go outside a dense field of loose ice, we were forced finally to turn back, and it was only by the hardest kind of work that the boats could be urged to windward through the chaos of tossing ice. Windward work through pack ice in heavy weather is perilous for skin boats. The large, flat-bottomed *umiak* pounds considerably forward, and if it should happen to come down with full force on an ice cake, there would be a disaster, complete and unavoidable. The more easily managed kayaks with their lighter load are not in nearly so much danger. Also, the kayak with its low freeboard goes to windward without much effort and does not drift to leeward. As an old canoeman, I could appreciate this point. I have pushed a kayak against a wind that would have blown a canoe out of the water, not without effort to be sure, but I got there.

Hansen, even though dressed in furs, was having a cold and uncomfortable time in the stern of the *umiak*. His wife was intensely afraid of kayak work and had never allowed him to try it. One of the finest of fellows, he had been many years a sailor, and a good one, in the old squarerigged ships. I was fortunate in having him in charge of the trip. Thank the Lord he could speak a little English.

For 18 hours we navigated, going ashore frequently to plan out the course ahead, circling some ice fields, penetrating others, and all the time working South toward the little Eskimo village of Isortok, where we planned to stay that night, if we could get into the shore there. At times we were outside the fringe of small rocky islands, perhaps five miles from the coast; at others we were close to the end of long peninsulas. The shallow bays were covered with young ice not quite strong enough to travel on, but too strong for boats to penetrate.

No one seemed to know the precise bay in which the village lay, but eventually, just as my great weariness began to seem unbearable, we spied a stream of black figures pouring out over the ice toward us from a deep fiord. We could not yet see the houses, but the inhabitants had seen us and were coming in full force to welcome us. Soon we were being assisted onto the ice with the greatest kindness and were asked to stay. Indeed, we were told we must stay, as a storm was surely coming. The American doctor, *nagorsak,* was something of a curiosity, and they would keep him awhile even if they had to conjure up a storm. I consented to stay, as both the crew and I seemed unfit to travel farther without rest, and I was assured that word would have come if the ship had arrived. My objection was that Holsteinsborg was only 15 miles away, and the ship might be ready to leave. I took the precaution to send two kayak men immediately to Holsteinsborg with letters to the Danish governor. I felt no doubt the storm would hold off for them if I could pay enough.

Fortunately there was a branch store at Isortok where we could get coffee, sugar, bread, cigars, etc. The trader, a fairly well-educated Greenlander, made us owners of his two-roomed frame house. The primus was started on the floor, and coffee made for all hands. We were nearly killed with kindness before morning, and the heat was murderous. One of the things a Greenlander knew to perfection was how to make a warm house. The sides were of turf, or, if of wood, were banked to the eaves with turf and grass. The entrance was through a tunnel ten feet long with a door at each end, so low that one had to crouch and scuffle along in a most undignified manner. Usually one encountered a cross dog or two and was lucky to get away with one's life. It was wise to try to entice the dogs out before entering, as they were not friendly toward strangers. These South Greenland dogs were as a rule more treacherous than that more close descendant of the white wolf, the Polar Eskimo dog.

For the first time during the whole long winter in South Greenland, the weather had become continuously cold. Usually by this time, the middle of April, the coast would be free from young ice, but now the north wind had brought an unprecedented cold snap. It almost seemed to me as one more attempt to stop me. It was 32 below at midnight.

We were slow in getting away the next morning. The warmth of heart and house was almost too good to exchange for a wintry sea. The whole village came with us to the launching a mile out on the ice. As the Eskimo would say: "The American-kayak-man-who-came-from-the-faraway-Inuit" was an object of much curiosity. My bear skin pants especially produced much excitement, for the *nanook*, the polar bear, is only a legend to these people. They were pointed at, felt of, and wondered at by these Eskimos, and barked at by the dogs, to my great discomfort. Every least movement of mine was watched, and some were laughed at, as I put my kayak in the water and wedged myself in.

It takes an appreciable time to get settled into the little 21-inch-wide kayak through the 18-inch hole in the middle of the deck. Neptune and Boreas must be invoked to keep quiet, courage summoned, and the craft placed in the water. One end of the long paddle is slipped under the straps just forward of the seat. The other extends out to sea and acts in a measure as a stabilizer. With one hand firmly grasping Greenland, a foot is cautiously placed in the opening, then two feet. One sits down, immediately grabs both rails, hopes no one is unkind enough to look, and shoves forward to safety. Once one is in, the position is not as uncomfortable as it seems, although the white man suffers somewhat from the habit of sitting in chairs. In a kayak, one's legs must be out straight.

We began to encounter new ice almost immediately, and for the rest of the day were reduced to a snail's pace. The *umiak* broke the way slowly, with a man out over either bow treading under and breaking up the thicker floes, while leaning over and holding onto the boat for dear life. The two kayaks followed in the wake. There was a rather dangerous stiffness to the ice, and I noticed a quite perceptible wearing of the sealskin at the waterline of the *umiak*. A long, low swell was rolling in from the sea, the ice bending in waves. We were in sight of the Holsteinsborg cliffs almost all day, fighting our way through, back and forth, wherever the ice seemed weaker, rather like in a sailboat tacking against a shifting wind. Several walrus pushed their huge heads up through the ice to look at our strange squadron, and seals and eider ducks were abundant.

Finally getting into a nest of small islands through which the tide was setting swiftly, we went ashore and were agreeably surprised to find open water ahead clear to the harbor. We stopped long enough to eat some ship biscuit and congratulate each other. With the Wilderness behind us and the Promised Land ahead, our hardships were forgotten. Two hours more and the goal of my four months' trip would be at hand. Another month would see me in Copenhagen and then New York, I hoped.

The last lap to harbor was at hand. I might use myself as hard as I pleased today. There would be no work tomorrow, and I resolved to carry on with what stamina I had left. The others sensed the race, and for awhile the oarsmen pushed their boat with tremendous power, shouting and rising from their seats at each stroke. I could gain slowly on them, but knowing they would soon tire, I was content just to hold my own. My real opponent was the other kayak man; skill I knew he had, but I strongly suspected that power and endurance lay with me.

Foot by foot, the *umiak* dropped back, as the men tired, and on we two sped, each holding a little in reserve for the last mile. A glance at my companion showed him shooting gracefully along with a smooth, even stroke, and with apparently no exertion; yet, unless I was mistaken, his chest was beginning to heave, and in spite of the cold, drops of sweat were running down his nose.

Gradually, I began to exert myself. His prow clung to mine with a dogged persistence. I still was saving myself a little. Suddenly we saw a man on a promontory a little way ahead. He was pointing the way into a small cove, across the mouth of which the swell was breaking heavily. Now was my chance. Putting every atom of force I could summon into each stroke, I dashed in on the top of the first roller, shooting a clear 50 yards into still water. The other kayak, only a few feet behind me, had missed my wave. I watched him come in, and together we slowly paddled to the landing, where Governor and Mrs. Binser, Pastor and Mrs. Frederiksen, and the whole population of Holsteinsborg were waiting for us. Soon the *umiak* came in, and we all were literally lifted from the boats by many kind hands.

XIII

Holsteinsborg and Onward April 22-June 20, 1917

IT WAS ON APRIL TWENTY-SECOND that I arrived at Holsteinsborg, not in January as Ek and I had anticipated. Happily the ship from Denmark, although expected and even long overdue, had not come in yet.

The Danish people were most hospitable to me, and fortunately all could speak some English. Governor Binser took me immediately to a small guest house, which he offered to Hansen and me for as long as we wished. A bath in a warm room was followed by dinner at the Governor's, with two Danish ladies. We had music, coffee and sweet cakes, a game of chess, generous toasts of schnapps and scotch, and then, clean sheets.

Hansen afterwards told me that my arrival had somewhat disappointed my new friends. They had come down to meet a man dressed in the elegant fur costume of the Polar Inuit and had found a tired and wet kayak man. I was dressed entirely in the waterproof sealskins of the South Greenland Inuit.

The route from Thule to Holsteinsborg was an established one, traveled by dogsled in moonlight and early spring sunlight, along smooth, landfast ice. One could generally ride the sledge. Tank, Allen, and Green had done it the previous year. This year had presented difficulties.

Every year, wherever water freezes in the fall and thaws in the spring, there is a time when the ice is unsafe, yet does not allow boating, except with modern icebreakers. It was this way, of course, in Greenland. The Eskimos there, many of whom lived on islands, and all of whom depended on the sea for transportation, be it by dogsled or boat, were prepared with enormous caches of food and blubber to tide them over the time when they would be immobilized.

This year, from Tasiussak, where we met our first South Greenland Inuit, to well south of Holsteinsborg, extraordinarily warm weather, followed by equally unusual cold, prolonged this period of immobilization, causing extreme hardship and hunger all up and down the coast. I could only hope that the friends I made all survived. I could not wait to see. I had to travel even when I was told one could not travel. The welfare of those I left behind at Etah as well as my personal reasons forced me to proceed. Because I went such roundabout ways, I figure I must have covered well over 1,500 American miles, and few of those riding the sledge.

The weather continued cold at Holsteinsborg, and when we arrived, two of the company boats had been out a week trying to reach some small settlements to the south. They had not been heard from and were overdue. To everyone's relief, they returned the following day, although ice had prevented one of them from reaching its destination. For twelve days new ice kept the *umiak* that had brought Hansen and the mail from returning to Agto. No one could remember ice forming like that in April. We had been fortunate to get in when we did.

The village of Holsteinsborg lies on the eastern shore of an almost landlocked harbor. To the north, sheltering it from wind, rises a huge cliff, some 1,200 feet high. This is, in nesting time, the abode of literally countless murres, from which the Eskimos take their annual toll by the use of their long-handled nets. Off the harbor mouth lie several islands of various sizes, and farther still one can see white surf breaking over rocks scarcely awash. Seal and walrus are out there, cod and halibut, occasionally white whale, and everywhere ducks. To the eastward, narrow valleys lead off toward smoother fields with herds of caribou, and back some 50 miles lies the border of the great Greenland icecap.

The Danish Government maintained a paternalistic policy toward the Greenlanders and Inuit, supplying the villages with a governor or trader, like the factor of the Hudson's Bay Company. In the larger places were small but good hospitals with a Greenlander nurse who had had some instruction in the hospitals of Copenhagen, sometimes a doctor, and usually a Lutheran minister. The stores themselves contained guns, ammunition, tobacco, coffee, sugar, flour, dishes, knives, cloth, etc., which were sold to the natives at a remarkably low price. The Eskimos in return sold their seal and walrus blubber, skins, and ivory to the government at a fair price, so all concerned fared well enough. In addition to this, the fisheries were worked during the summer by the trader, giving occupation to many of the natives. The Greenland trade was a Danish Crown Monopoly, but I understand was not a source of revenue. This monopoly did not at that time extend to the Cape York-Smith Sound district, the land of the Polar Inuit, where Knud and Peter traded.

Many of the Eskimo houses in Holsteinsborg were of double-walled frame construction, with a cement foundation, warm and clean inside and neatly painted outside. Others were as squalid as can be imagined — damp, dirty, foul smelling, and vermin infested. The houses of the Europeans were invariably clean, warm, and of an admirably solid construction. Every home had a piano, and good cheer and hospitality were the keynotes. Enforced separation from children during their education in Denmark was naturally looked on with sorrow, but I think, on the whole, these people were happier and more contented, and had a more wholesome home life, than us of the big cities. Certainly the church at Holsteinsborg was better filled than any in American communities I know of.

The three weeks I spent there were not really a hardship. Hansen and I were awakened in the morning by the smell of fresh-roasted coffee, and we would hustle out of bed to get some, but before we could, the maid would bring small cups of very black, bitter, delicious Danish coffee. Then we would go to the house of the Governor for breakfast: oatmeal, more coffee, coffee bread, and ale. The best home-brewed ale I ever tasted was always on the table. Mrs. Binser was a Greenlander and a beautiful girl. At the end of every meal, Governor Binser marched around the table and gave her a hearty kiss. After breakfast the Governor and I visited the hospital where two patients were in bed, one with typhoid, one with scurvy, and where every day we held a large outpatient clinic. Dinner was at two, and there was always an abundance of meat, fish, bread, jellies, etc., followed by the ever-present schnapps and coffee.

I had quite a lot of time on my hands and improved it by learning to be a better kayak man. There were some experts in town, the kind who could roll over and come up on the other side, and repeat it, over and over. They taught me to upset my kayak and get upright again. I learned without much trouble. They said that no kayak man was fit to go off by himself unless he could recover from an upset.

I was introduced to an Eskimo chess player. We played hour after hour, with intervals for coffee, and I knew I was expected to exert myself and play well, which I did. He was a dwarf, short, humped back, large head, probably had rickets as a child. He had to have a hassock on his chair. He was a good player but knew nothing about the opening plays, so I tried different ones and would get a little bit ahead of him and stay there. Although he lost time after time, he never expressed any disappointment. He was a good sport.

At five we had more coffee and schnapps. Supper was at seven. In the evenings we invariably met with either the Binsers or the Fredericksens, with music, black coffee, sandwiches, and possibly a little scotch. What more could one desire than such friendship, warmth, and plenty?

Home and one's own.

Those three weeks passed almost as if in a dream, yet were a wearisome burden to me. Daily we watched from the lookout place for signs of a ship. The *Hans Egede* was so long overdue there was some thought that because of the war she might not come at all.

The endless days at Etah and then at Umanak were brought to mind. Had I fought my way south only to be balked again? Day after day I worked my kayak southward, seeing smudges that turned to clouds and grey shapes that became icebergs, and as often I came back sore at heart and savage at the great museum whose contract I had trusted, at their failure to send a well-found ship. A three-masted auxiliary schooner indeed! [The *Cluett*.] And with no man on board who had ever been in those waters! The following year a ship with insufficient coal! [The *Danmark*] Both too late in the season!

I grew bitter. I was bitter about Mac and Hovey. Mac did enjoy and understand the Arctic. He also enjoyed being boss. To Hovey the expedition was just a vehicle for his own advancement. So it seemed to me. The great purposes of the expedition to which I had devoted myself for four years became a will-o'-the-wisp that faded before my eyes. Would getting home prove equally elusive? Crocker Land was a mirage; would every sign of a ship here also be a mirage?

There were some dories in the bay that wrecked Gloucester fishermen had sold to the Danes. The dories were large and in good condition. My obstinate resolve was such that I decided, in case the Danish ship did not come, that I would rig sails in one of them, cross Davis Strait, make for Baffin Land, and work my way down to the Labrador coast. I had not walked and paddled almost the whole length of Greenland just to spend another year there. I would take my chances with the gales and ice of the northern sea.

We had retired about ten o'clock the night of May twelfth and were having our last cigar in bed, when a great shouting began from the Eskimo houses: "*Umiakswa, umiakswa!*" Mingled with the outcry we heard the shrill whistle of a steamer and the rattle of chain running through the hawse-pipe. The *Hans Egede* had arrived.

The ship brought the news that the United States had finally declared war on April sixth. I had mail from Bangor, but the Museum sent no word, no letter of credit, nothing. Surely they should have expected some member of the expedition to be there. I had no passport. My money was about gone. After some delay, the Captain fortunately agreed to take me as passenger, and three days later we sailed in a fresh wind and rough sea for Godthaab and the Faroe Islands en route to Copenhagen.

The *Hans Egede* was an old steel ship, 150 feet overall, built for rough ice work, and, for that reason, without a keel. We had a full cargo of seal oil, partly in barrels, but with a small amount in iron tanks. The service was perfect, and we eight passengers well cared for, except that because of the lack of a keel, the vessel rolled surprisingly. The cabins all opened off the dining saloon, and there was no fresh air. Of course there were no bathing facilities, but we could wash down in the warm engine room with buckets of hot water, soap, and a scrub brush. I did not get seasick easily, but with the stench of those who did, combined with that of the seal oil, my appetite often failed. I met a Dr. Andersen aboard who played a good game of chess, and for the first time in four years I met my match regularly.

Off the end of Greenland, the heavy east coast ice met us and turned us aside for a day. The grim and jagged coast of Iceland loomed on our left, and we stopped at Reykjavik for news of the war. New birds arrived, and soon we sighted the forlorn, dismal cliffs of the Faroes. A sparrow came aboard. Thorshavn might be any small New England fishing port, changed just a little, with the menfolk wearing knee pants and curious hats. U-boats were about, and the fishing fleet was in harbor, as several boats had been sunk lately. It was Sunday. I could get no clothes, and not even a haircut. Finally I went up to the British Consul's in my Greenland skin costume. He could give me no passport of any kind, and advised me not to try to reach Denmark. On the other hand, he advised me that without a passport I would be arrested as a spy if I went to England. I didn't like the latter alternative and decided to go on and chance a German ship in the Skagerrak. The wireless station would not take my message to New York without being paid, so I left my last penny there and went back aboard the steamer again. I have not paid the ferryman yet.

> CABLEGRAM; HUNT TO AMERICAN MUSEUM OF NATURAL HISTORY:
>
> MACMILLAN COMER SMALL HOVEY ETAH DANMARK NORTH STAR BAY EKBLAW GODHAVN HUNT HANS EGEDE ARRANGE CREDIT PASSPORT COPENHAGEN THROUGH AMERICAN MINISTER.

After three hours waiting, we steamed out of the little harbor and headed east for the coast of Norway, well above the submarine zone. Two nights later I saw Europe for the first time. The lights on the coast were shining kindly at all the world. Small fishing sloops were about their business even as at home. And a short way to the south lay the *Lusitania* with its thousand dead. Might we also be sunk without a trace? By daylight the whole coast lay exposed: islands, bay, lighthouse, and sails without number. Two more nights and the first great light marking the entrance to the Skagerrak was blinking through the mists of the Danish shore. Danish ships were often being stopped by German destroyers here. Had this happened to the *Hans Egede,* I would have been taken and put to work in Germany, but no destroyer found us. The next morning we were greeted by an airplane patrolling the channel for possible submarines, and we went right into Copenhagen without interruption.

We docked about noon on my thirty-ninth birthday, June 1, 1917. I understood but a little Danish. I had a full beard, badly needed a haircut, and was lousy. I had on Eskimo sealskin clothes and had no money to buy others. Apparently in spite of my cable from the Faroes, the Museum had not seen fit to have me met in Copenhagen. The day was hot, and as I watched my friends disembark and go up the dock I confess to a feeling that I was not out of the woods yet.

I determined to appeal to the American Minister, Mr. Egan, and accordingly inquired the way to a telephone and asked for the American Legation. The ship's captain gave me money to pay for the telephone. I had some trouble telling who I was and where I had come from, but once they understood, my difficulties were over. Soon an attache came for me in a taxi. I was whisked uptown to a clothing store, given unlimited credit, outfitted from top to toe, and taken to a hotel. There was no red tape about this business. My bills were paid, and I had money in my pocket without even having to sign my name. My first purchase was a copy of *The Ladies Home Journal* that I found in a newsstand, for the advertisements.

I received a cable from the Museum that the *Neptune* with Peary's former captain, Bob Bartlett, in command, would leave soon for Etah with a year's provisions aboard. They wanted to know if I thought it necessary! If this same ship had been sent in the first place, something like $100,000 would have been saved, and two years' privation for those left in the north avoided.

Minister Egan was overwhelmed with work but saw me fitted out with a passport immediately. He personally saw to it that I got a first-class ticket on the first steamer home: the SS *United States* of the Scandinavian-American Line, leaving in five days from Norway.

I went by ferry and train to Christiania [Oslo] and awaited the steamer there. From that port, our route lay outside the submarine zone, northward up the coast as far as Bergen, and thence westward to America. Crossing the Skagerrak, I had been well hidden in the hold, as Germans had searched the previous ferry for Americans, but the passage through the German blockade on the *United States* was uneventful. We slipped into New York the twentieth of June, within two weeks of an absence of four years.

There on the quay was my fair Marion, unchanged. As I saw her hesitate, I realized how weatherbeaten I looked, and that she had never seen me with a beard. Then she threw herself at me and said, "I'll always know your eyes." I did not hear her. That I had grown quite deaf was unknown to her. It did not matter.

No longer would I "go-go-go away from here!"

Epilogue

In Uncle Rich's Letter to Hal's father in 1913 (see Chapter 1), he wrote, "... my mind is most on what will come after. Will the associations at the New York Museum lead to some dispensation there? Will the Arctic experience help in starting again 'the common task, the trivial round?' Or does the call of the wild never lessen its temperature ..."

In the summer of 1917 the *Neptune* brought out the men remaining at Etah: MacMillan, Jot Small, Dr. Hovey, and Captain Comer, along with the equipment and collections of the expedition. They picked up Ek at Godhavn, South Greenland, and all came home safely.

Captain Comer talked with Marion, and here is her report to the family on what he had to say:

> Captain Comer: I dare not tell you what I think of your husband, or you would think I was trying to flatter. Hal is one of Nature's noblemen, and you won't find one in a thousand like him. In my report his name comes first, and he is head and shoulders above them all. I place him and Dr. Tanquary above the others. He has helped me a lot, and not only that, but his personality and encouragement meant a great deal, being such a contrast to some of the others.
>
> The whole expedition was founded on selfishness. Peary reached a little too far, wished to see land, thought he did, and claimed it, resulting in the Crocker Land fiasco ... MacMillan used the expedition as his plaything ... I told the museum to dig a big hole, bury the whole thing, and put stones on top of it.
>
> Dr. Hovey was penny-wise and pound-foolish ... He paid poorly and did not treat the people right ... The museum contract he prepared for the men to sign was childish, unfair, and improperly prepared.
>
> The *Cluett* was a sailing vessel, not fit for a relief ship, and not properly prepared in many respects. The *Danmark* was not only a relief ship, but also had taken on two tons of graphite to deliver. If it had not been for that, it could have gone to Etah and returned before being caught in the ice. The last two years were the hardest, and they were unnecessary.
>
> Make a few friends and keep them. I never shall let Hal go. Once when we were on a trip alone, and the food was short, we had some words about the bread. There was a little soft white bread, and I wanted him to have it. Finally he looked at me and said sternly, "Eat that or starve." I ate it and shall never forget it. Now you have him, Mrs. Hunt, stick together through thick and thin. He is a wonder.

Hal agreed with Captain Comer about the leadership of the expedition, and unfortunately his association with the American Museum of Natural History also soon became an adversary relationship. Immediately upon his return, he reported in person to President Osborn of the museum, whom he admired, but who, he felt, was hoodwinked by MacMillan and misled by Dr. Hovey. He also requested additional pay for eighteen months' care of Dr. Hovey and the crew of the *Cluett*, since they were not covered by the contract, and for his prolonged stay in Greenland due to the inadequacies of the relief ships.

Hal and Marion had no money; she had not even been able to pay for a typewriter she had bought in June, just before Hal's return. A $500 check for the services rendered Dr. Hovey and the crew, and a July letter from President Osborn, to the effect that yes, indeed, he thought Hal should receive further compensation, were much appreciated. The $500 helped see him through intensive training in urology at the Peter Bent Brigham and Massachusetts General Hospitals. But when, after consultation with Dr. Hovey, President Osborn wrote that Hal's prolonged stay had been voluntary, that the Committee recommended no further payments, and that a report on Hal by MacMillan and Hovey would lead to hard feelings, Hal blew up. He wrote a long and angry letter to the Honorary Committee, Crocker Land Expedition, dated 16 May, 1918:

> . . . When I read my contract I said to myself, the Museum is square. I had signed it unread on that basis. When the *Cluett* came north I said, the Museum is square, but someone has made a mistake. When the *Cluett* ran short of food I said the same thing. But when the Museum says my prolonged stay was "voluntary" I believe someone has said a dishonest thing. Let me attempt to prove it . . .
>
> I had direct and explicit orders from MacMillan to stay at North Star Bay until the arrival of the relief ship [the *Danmark*]. These orders have been in the Museum since I returned in June, 1917 . . .
>
> The contract also provides that MacMillan shall be the sole leader of the expedition and responsible for it until its return to New York . . . Therefore, I was obeying orders, and President Osborn is wrong in saying that my prolonged stay was "voluntary."
>
> Again, when the *Cluett* broke out of the ice in 1916, she was short of food. She had been serving all winter less than two-thirds regular seamens' rations. She was dragging a large useless propeller as well. No one will urge that she was properly fitted for the dangers and delays incident to Arctic service. Yet because I did not disobey orders, and come home on an unsafe ship, the Museum denies me compensation.
>
> Now I have at hand a letter from Pres. Osborn dated April 25 in which he writes as follows: "I have discouraged a report which would lead only to hard feeling. In case you think it is your duty to report, it would be necessary for me to submit your report first to Mr. MacMillan and to Dr. Hovey, which would give rise to their reports on your management of your division." What now threatens! Dr. Hovey again is to play bogey man, to scare off a poverty-stricken unimportant country doctor. Luckily for me I have kept Pres. Osborn's letter of July the 17, 1917, in which he says: "You will be glad to know that we have received the letters and reports

> from the various members of the expedition, which you mailed in Copenhagen. These reports confirm the good news brought out by you of the health of the party. Dr. Hovey speaks in the highest terms of the services rendered by you to the members of the Crocker Land Expedition and to the relief expd. and especially of your efficient care of Mr. Peter Freuchen. I am particularly pleased with the assistance you thus gave to Mr. Rasmussen." But it seems that Dr. Hovey can sing another song, on request, perhaps an indefinite number, and can give a "report which will lead only to hard feeling." (in Pres. Osborn's words). Why such a report anyway.
>
> MacMillan and I disagree on many points, we have said hard things about each other, but I think I know that he agrees with me on all or about all the points I have raised here.
>
> Then too it would be only fair to ask the other members of the Crocker Land Expedition. Ask Captain Comer also. He is a man of large experience and has a first hand knowledge of the matter. I have not written to any of them about this report, that they might be uninfluenced by me. I reserve the right to do so however.
>
> On April 25 Pres. Osborn writes me: "We did our very best and spared no pains and no expense to take care of our entire party and bring them home safely." Now I ask you, was it best to send a sailing vessel north after the Crocker Land Party? Was it then, and would it be now, good practice?
>
> Was it doing the best, and sparing no pains, to send such a vessel, or any vessel, inadequately provisioned?
>
> Finally, if this committee cannot agree that I should be further compensated, I ask for the matter to be put in the hands of such a man as Theodore Roosevelt, or Chas. A. Hughes. They are wholly disinterested, and I would abide by the decision of either. All I ask is fair treatment.

This from my unassuming father, and a doctor who would not send a bill!

Hal's letter sparked an equally angry letter from Dr. Hovey to President Osborn. He maintained that Ekblaw had had the authority to give permission, as he had done, for Hal to go out on the *Cluett* in the summer of 1916. He also charged that Hal was disloyal to the expedition and its leader and was a general troublemaker, that he openly and unreasonably criticised the expedition, was active in spreading exaggerated statements regarding the trading in foxskins done by the expedition, and even went so far as to tell the Danes [Rasmussen and Freuchen] that MacMillan was a hypocrite and wholly unreliable. He wrote how Hal's attitude on his journey through southern Greenland was that the Museum had "barrels of money" and could be "mulcted to any amount" for the expenses of getting out.

That Hal told his friends, Rasmussen and Freuchen, just what he thought of MacMillan, his trading in foxskins, and his leadership of the expedition, I do not doubt, but the record shows complete loyalty to the expedition itself and scrupulous attention to the terms of the contract. As for his alleged extravagance with the Museum's money on his journey through southern Greenland, his Field Notes show a meticulous concern not to spend a single kroner more than necessary.

In any case, as Mac accurately and generously pointed out in a letter dated May 13, 1918, to President Osborn, Hal's attitude had nothing to do with the question of further compensation.

> Doctor's claim for further compensation is based upon his enforced stay in the Arctic regions, not upon my report upon his work or his relations to the Expedition.
>
> My orders to Doctor Hunt to remain at North Star Bay and await the arrival of the relief ship were given with the approval of Doctor Hovey . . .

The orders referred to had been written on Jan. 3, 1916, and stated, "You are to remain at the sub-station at Umanak under the command of Mr. Elmer Ekblaw until the arrival of the relief ship [the *Danmark*] in July and August of this year, or until further orders."

The *Danmark* having been frozen in, Hal received his further orders in December of 1916 and left by dog sledge accordingly. Nonetheless, a May 17, 1918, letter from Mr. Sherwood of the Crocker Land Committee to President Osborn repeated that Hal had stayed on voluntarily since he had been under Ek's command at Umanak and had had his permission to sail on the *Cluett*. Considering this affair, Hal wanted nothing more to do with either the museum or the expedition. It was the last straw.

Hal put it all behind him and set a new course, with his profession as the lodestar. He settled in Bangor, where, gradually building up a successful practice, he inaugurated the Urological Section at the Eastern Maine General Hospital, of which his father had been a founder, and ran one of the first Public Health Clinics for venereal disease in the State of Maine.

Upon Hal's return from the north, life started afresh also for Marion and me; for Marion, who had been wondering what reunion would mean, when the *United States* docked in New York; for me when the *Camden* docked in Bangor, and my father strode through the cheering crowd on the wharf to gather me into his arms. When Marion first saw Hal, she could hardly find him behind his beard, but he quickly shaved it off, and there he was, her Hal. Soon he was writing, "I love you more as the years go by . . . Both you and Ruth seem to me to be such wonderfully splendid girls," and she wrote Uncle Rich, "He is a star. I am deeper in love than ever, thank God."

While Hal practiced medicine in Bangor, Marion administered a small private hospital for a few years, continued to teach for a time in Bangor High School, tutored young people headed for college, learned and taught lip reading to help Hal with his deafness, and taught and wrote a booklet on contract bridge.

They never did have the longed-for son, but Hal found a nine-year-old little girl who did her level best to match her stride to his. I found a father who took me cruising, camping in the deep woods, and snowshoeing on winter picnics with great fires in hollow trees, one who told me vivid stories of blizzards and polar bears. At home there were sometimes hard words and tension, while I sat silent, seething, and insecure. Hal was never easy to live with, and Marion always found him baffling, while only gradually did I come to understand both. Thus was my relationship formed with the father whom I had not remembered very well. I was unsure of myself, in awe, fearful of displeasing him, and also fearful of what dangers he might lead me into. Yet there was excitement, a snug security in his strength, a certainty of his love, and I adored him.

Although Hal spoke often of his experiences and of his Eskimo friends, no longer did "the world's white roof tree" call him. In his leisure time he was content to roam Maine's wilderness and sail its coast. He found where the moose yarded high up on Traveller Mountain, and where the best holding ground was in harbors from Boston to Campobello. He played chess and he read widely.

Hal read all he could find about the North and about the Polar Inuit whom he had loved so well. He learned that many of his companions had died of accidents or of the 1918 flu, which decimated the tribe, but some twenty years after he had left the north, the Danish government appointed a doctor to the district of Thule.

In *Eskimo Doctor* (W.W. Norton and Co., Inc., New York, 1948), Dr. Aage Gilberg, the first State appointed doctor there, wrote of Christmas, 1938, among the Polar Inuit, "In Europe people are full of peace and good will at Christmas only long enough to give a brief vision of how life ought to be lived. In Thule the Christmas spirit prevails on weekdays too, and there really is good will and peace among men." His district was the same Hal had covered, from Cape Melville on the south to Anoritok on the north, though he never traveled north of Siorapaluk, about 65 miles south of Etah. He found no vitamin deficiency, no cancer, no appendicitis, but tuberculosis had worked its way up from South Greenland.

In 1960-1961 Jean Malaurie spent a year in the Thule district, with his headquarters at Siorapaluk. In *The Last Kings of Thule* (Thomas Y. Crowell Co., New York, 1956), he wrote of Hal's friends Ootah and Poodaloona, and of Peary's sons and grandson. He called Nookapingwa, the young man Hal wrote of who had had bad manners and drank all the whisky, as "the only man to know Ellesmere Land at all well." Malaurie, deeply disturbed by the disrupting influences of a shoddy civilization impinging on the Eskimo culture, learned to his delight that the Polar Eskimos had decided on their own initiative to move their village of Thule, at North Star Bay, cheek by jowl with Thule Air Force Base, to the Eskimo settlement of Kanak, 125 miles north. Like their forefathers, the nomadic Inuit were once again on the move, searching for a better life.

These accounts gave Hal hope for his friends and their descendants, a hope which still seems well-founded. John J. Putman wrote in the September, 1975, *National Geographic*, "Greenland Feels the Winds of Change," that the Polar Inuit have remained aloof from the smothering comforts of South Greenland, where the Greenlanders, for there are few true Eskimos left, struggle to find their identity between the old hunting culture and the modern technological age. The northern tribe has a hospital and a school. The incidence of tuberculosis is way down. The babies wear paper diapers, but the men wear polar bear trousers and caribou *kooletahs*. They have great sledges and huge dogs, and hunt narwhal with kayaks. There are 600 Polar Inuit, and hunting families are moving north from Upernavik.

Even as our way of life has encroached on theirs, the Polar Inuit have persevered in the old ways, aided in this by the Danish Government. Now, in 1979, one wonders what Greenland's new independence from Denmark will mean, but as long as the Polar Inuit can hold onto the great qualities of self-reliance, originality, and kindliness that Hal found in them, their physical survival and cultural integrity seem assured.

The years went on. To Hal's joy, the discovery of penicillin made vast inroads on venereal disease. After 30 years, the clinic became outdated and was closed. Hal was restless, and, as he had told his father, he intended to use his training the best he could as long as he lived.

In 1913, the *Boston Sunday Herald* had run an advertisement, "Wanted, a doctor for the Crocker Land Expedition, sailing in 6 wks., to be gone 2 yrs.," and yes, they had wanted Hal.

In 1952 a *Bangor Daily News* ad, "Wanted at once, a doctor for the Red Cross Blood Mobile Unit in Maine," caught his attention, and for a year he traveled all over the state. It seemed to me as if everywhere he went he was an old friend. Donors flocked in, but a mobile setup proved unnecessarily expensive and was discontinued.

In 1954 it was an ad in the *Journal of the American Medical Association*, "Wanted, an adventurous doctor for part time island practice." What island, or where, Hal did not know, but, though 76 years old, he wanted this job. It turned out that the Maine Seacoast Mission had put in the ad for Swan's Island, Maine, whose coast and harbors my father knew well, and again, yes, they wanted him. Hal had been a country doctor, an arctic doctor, a city specialist, and in his old age he would be an island's general practitioner.

Swan's Island, a large lobsterman's island at the entrance to Blue Hill Bay, has three townships: Swan's Island, Minturn, and Atlantic. Father also served the town of Frenchboro, on outer Long Island, separated from Swan's by several miles of open ocean. In those days one went to Swan's Island by lobster boat, yacht, or mailboat, and for those who had no boat it was mostly by mailboat, the *Sea Wind*, a tough, seaworthy craft, but not particularly comfortable. Boarding and landing were by slippery perpendicular ladders at the end of windswept docks down to or up from a heaving deck. On stormy days one could relax safely only on the cabin floor, braced in a corner.

Shortly after his arrival, Father wrote a medical colleague in Bangor:

> I am a dentist, an obstetrician, a pediatrician. Among other things I do physical therapy, syringe ears, revive a drowning man, treat heart trouble, asthma, and a boy with a nail in his foot. And these troubles do not come singly but in bunches . . . My office is a corner of our home. House not so hot. Toilet flushed by pail water. No bath. I have lived in worse but Marion not . . ."

To the fact that this move would be a hardship for my mother, my father paid little heed. Perhaps no one, and certainly not Hal, ever realized how much he needed her, or how difficult this uprooting was for her. At the age of 74 she put home and friends in mothballs and set up housekeeping anew among total strangers on an isolated island. The house, cold and drafty, lacked amenities, and its water supply depended on rain collected in a cistern in the cellar. The toilet was under the stairs, and one couldn't quite stand upright. There was no bathtub. This my mother could not take, and since the only place that could accommodate a tub was a corner of a room that had always served as a living room, she eventually put a tub in the living room.

The view from the house was magnificent, however. It looked down on Burnt Coat Harbor, always occupied by dozens of white lobster boats, and in summer often filled with cruising yachts. Beyond, out through the harbor entrance, rolled the great swells of the Atlantic Ocean, unfurling into surf on reefs and island shores.

Hal was in his element. His seafaring neighbors and their self-reliant wives and children were his kind of people. He put himself on call day and night, seven days a week. He slept in the hall outside his office, with the street light shining through the window on his white hair, visible and available to all. A touch on his shoulder woke him, and he would plug in his hearing aid. So that he could always be found in the daytime he would leave notes on the office door: "Gone to deliver Lemoine baby"; "Fishing at Goose Pond;" "By canoe from Carrying Place to Seal Cove, back by foot". In his canoe he circumnavigated the island and visited smaller islands, much to the consternation of his new friends. Whenever his canoe was sighted, lobstermen's radio telephones began crackling and home phones ringing as they alerted each other to keep an eye on him. He rented land for a vegetable garden from a man who plowed it with a horse and an ox. He explored island forests, where he studied the habits of birds and wild animals, he dug for Indian relics in the shell heaps, and he discovered abandoned house foundations and old granite quarries.

Both Marion and Hal became very fond of the islanders, who watched over the daily welfare of their doctor and his wife just as Hal watched over their medical needs. If my mother and father had strange ways much was forgiven them, for they were from "off island."

Father had hoped to spend the rest of his years on the island, but his legs became unsteady and his eyesight poor. He and Mother returned to their home in Bangor in 1960. Kind friends took him for drives, and even with failing eyesight his incredible memory guided them over back roads, past storied farms, and into territory new to the drivers. It was during these last years that he gave two television interviews and taped some of his Arctic experiences.

A few months before his death from pneumonia, on July 17, 1967, a solicitous friend asked what he would do if his wife predeceased him. He answered: "I'd get a boat."

Index